57 Days

The Wait for a New Heart
Sparks a Spiritual Journey
of Faith and Love

Pam Morris-Walton

ISBN 978-1-0980-2899-2 (paperback)
ISBN 978-1-0980-3901-1 (hardcover)
ISBN 978-1-0980-2900-5 (digital)

Christian Faith Publishing, Inc.
832 Park Avenue
Meadville, PA 16335
www.christianfaithpublishing.com

Printed in the United States of America

Contents

Introduction

I needed a new heart, not a stent or a pacemaker, but a heart, or I was not going to live. I could die. I didn't know where the new heart was going to come from or when it was going to come. I've been all over the world as a Gospel artist, radio host, wife, mother, and friend. But in the midst of a busy life, the greatest battle of my life was upon me. It was the search for a *new heart* that would replace the existing heart that was in my body.

God brought me through many situations before, but never had I experienced a challenge like this, and despite these personal victories, this was the biggest ever that would challenge my faith and leave me relying on something bigger than myself: God.

I no longer had control of my life. And this was scary for a woman who had strong faith but didn't have the answer to a problem that threaten to take my life.

For over three decades, I was a radio host who helped thousands of listeners with spiritual guidance with my music and inspirational words. As a mother, I was always quick to give advice to my sons about life, love, and people. Now it was me who needed help. The words that I said helped so many.

I recall being in a restaurant and the entire family thanked me and said, "You don't know how your words helped me." I am now blessed to receive what I have given others. I received lots of support from family and close family friends, but the only person who could give me the victory was God."

I had nowhere to turn to but God.

A new journey was about to begin, and I had no idea how it was going to turn out with all my faith being questioned. It was a journey that had its highs and lows, some good, and some bad days.

I think if life wanted to mess with me, it could have come up with a better way than taking my heart. I am a busy professional woman who is always on the go and always striving to help others achieve their goals and dreams. But now I was faced with a life-threatening goal that I had no idea how it would be accomplished.

It started with a single stop at Elmhurst Memorial Hospital. I was short of breath. My strength was in God, with lots of love from my family, and my close friends. My world narrowed. What once gave me so much pleasure is gone but how long? But as it turned out, my faith is still very much with me more than before.

Dr. Martin Luther King Jr. said, "Faith is taking the first step even when you don't see the whole staircase."

Dr. King was right.

I took the first step not seeing the whole staircase.

In Jeremiah 30:17, it reads, "'For I will restore health unto thee, and I will heal thee of thy wounds,' saith the Lord." KJV.

I'm taken back after reading this passage of Scripture in my Bible I keep near my bed on the left table stand. It was really speaking right to me, and that day happened in my life. Am I going to die? Death is nonnegotiable. I have grandkids. I'm a newlywed.

57 Days is a book I wrote for persons that know someone or personally have had a medical challenge or life-threatening situation with their heart. As you will read in the pages, I've written to never have been sick beyond a cold or flu like symptoms, and I find myself being told, "You need a heart." A voice took residence in my brain and said, "Tell your story."

I have always loved my walk through my life! I'm a West Virginia native born in Charleston, West Virginia, on December 20 in the year of our Lord! I was raised twelve miles away from Charleston Kankakee Hospital in Saint Albans, West Virginia. In my early years of growing up on Redd's Hill, many memories will forever be with me. The name Redds' Hill was later changed to Rosedale Drive in the 1980's right off old route 35. Up that curvy one lane road, you would see where I lived in a very lovely home for nearly nineteen years.

Redd's Hill was originally a predominately minority community where most of the residents were educators at local public schools, professors at West Virginia State College and owned family businesses. Home of my great-grandfather's general store, who also built my aunts Church which still stand today and my grandfather's shoe repair shop.

And the very first school I attended (Tackett Creek School) at six years of age had been torn down, and homes are built on that property today.

Maybe my first school was actually Sunday School at Aunt Mabel's Church in Saint Albans, West Virginia. Good lessons learned. I sat on the front row at the left side.

My educational training started at Tackett Creek, later St. Albans Junior High, and then St. Albans High to West Virginia State University. I was later blessed to birth two incredible, remarkable sons, John and Kenneth. I had watched my eldest son John (my tennis pro) and Kenneth (former United States Navy Lt. commander, aviator) develop into amazing adults and have beautiful families and bless me with talented, remarkable grandchildren.

For years, I've served as Interfaith Liaison to multiple clergy, pastors, bishops, and apostles throughout the City of Chicago for years and served an incredible United States House of Representatives congressmen and two outstanding gubernatorial candidates for the State of Illinois. I became a radio host/announcer. That includes more than four dozen years on radio every Sunday morning, sharing inspiring uplifting songs with a dose of hope and inspiration to countless listeners.

I'm a 2006 *Stellar Award Announcer of the Year* recipient. I'm also an emcee who introduced more choirs, singers, and groups than I can count. As an authority on Gospel music, I had recorded two Gospel albums and was recognized as an international gospel consultant. I was an advisor and program coordinator where I served in the City of Chicago Mayor's Office of Special Events Office on the eighth floor for twenty years being responsible for over twenty-five hundred Gospel artists performing on stage in the City of Chicago's downtown Grant and Millilumen Park.

I created, coordinated, and emceed for twenty years in the City of Chicago's Mayor Richard M. Daley's Annual Dr. Martin Luther King Jr. Interfaith Breakfast featuring such influential speakers as Dr. King's daughter, Rev. Bernice King; Dr. King's son, Martin Luther King III; ambassador Andrew Young, Father Michael Pfleger, Rev. Dr. Otis Moss Sr., and my pastor, Dr. Horace E. Smith, MD.

I retired from the City of Chicago in June 2009. I am remembering this post in the June 30, 2009, Chicago Defender newspaper:

> After two decades of helping the city bring some of the biggest names in the Gospel industry to Grant and (later) Millennium parks downtown. The walls in her South

Side home tell the real story of her success and adoration around the city and world-wide. The plethora of plagues, certificates and photos with high-profile dignitaries including U.S. presidents and South African President Nelson Mandela, and with famous Gospel recording artists, show how deeply entrenched her work as an ambassador for the city and the mayor Pam Morris was. And it is a clear indicator of just how much she loves Gospel music.

✳ In 2006, I authored a short story titled "Lessons Learned from Aunt Mabel and so much more." She left me at the age of ninety-one in Saint Albans, West Virginia, and pastored the Apostolic Free Church of God for sixty years.

✳ I also served on the Grammy Board of Governors of the National Academy of Recording Arts & Sciences Chicago Chapter. I'm a recipient of numerous awards including the *2010 Who's Who in Black Chicago Award, 2010 City of Chicago Appreciation Award, 2012 National Council of Negro Women Media Award*, and a *2014 HistoryMaker*.

My mind also took me back to the multiple trips to Rome and Perugia, Italy, to the Umbria Jazz Festival, touring with Gospel choirs, soloists, groups, and ensembles twenty-six times. I remember The Fisk University Jubilee Singers who were the only group that sang; it appeared all the time. They sang on the tour bus, sitting in the hotel lobby, or in the dressing rooms during breakfast, lunch, dinner, and of course, at the standing room only *sold out* concerts. What a pleasure to host The Fisk University Jubilee Singers twice in Italy.

I remember Gospel artist LaShun Pace and jazz art-ist Dianne Reeves so well, singing a Gospel duet together! I introduced so many performers for over twelve years who sang before sold out audiences every time and in wide open city squares filled with thousands of individuals. It was delightful, and everyone wanted more!

And years ago as an international Gospel consultant, I had provided services to a diverse list of entertainment venues that included the Gospel and Soul Easter Festival in Terni, Italy; The Tree of Life Gospel event in Durbin, South Africa; The New Orleans Jazz & Heritage Festival; and was the lead ambassador for American Heart Association Power to end Stroke Most Powerful Voices Gospel Tour.

And years later as you will read in the *first* chapter, my life changed; however, God chose me to be one of *his miracles!* I live with the words from the Holy Bible written in Philippians 4:13, "I can do all things through Christ which strengtheneth me." KJV.

Happy reading.

Chapter 1

A Day I Will Never Forget

In February 2016, I was diagnosed with *congestive heart failure*. The only thing I was thinking about was, *What does this mean?* It's my eldest son John's forty-fifth birthday. Kenneth is my youngest. I got the surprise of my life. I was sitting in the emergency room (Elmhurst Hospital). I was short of breath. A lady named Barbara, I believe, called for a wheelchair. I was thinking to myself, *A wheelchair? Certainly not for me. I can walk. Someone isn't going to push me around in a wheelchair. I can walk.* The tables turned on me, and the journey wasn't easy. Some dark uncertain blink days. *This was how my story unfolded.*

It's *early* in the morning, and as I look out the window, it was too nice of a day to be inside. Looking through the windshield, I saw patches of blue clouds coating the sky. I was dressed in a pair of black cotton slacks, red, black, and white long sleeve stripped high-collared blouse covering my black camisole with a black-beaded belt wrapped around my waist while chewing Wrigley double mint gum. We were headed down the highway to visit my mom in Dunbar, West Virginia, Nursing Facility on Tuesday, February 23, 2016. I didn't make that trip that day nor the next day.

Let me tell you, I certainly can't tell my mom, not in Mom's current condition about what I found out was going on with me. Mom's ill. Quite ill.

I will always remember when visiting Mom in West Virginia about my *private* stop on MacCorkle Avenue in Charleston for my order of just one Shoney's world-famous hot fudge cake with vanilla ice cream between freshly baked layers of Shoney's famous chocolate cake covered in hot fudge dripping off all four edges covered in hot fudge sauce with whipped cream topping and a cherry. Humm. I never had the whipped cream.

I wondered if Harry is still there. I remember. Harry kept filling my glass with water and delivering saucers full of cut lemons, of course, at my request.

Some days later, I was still thinking after several tests, conversations, and prescriptions for four different meds to be taken daily for three months. I can't crush or ignore this. Now I have *advanced congestive heart failure*. It's not just difficult; it is painfully difficult.

How do I deal with this unimaginable news? My eyes watered. I know I am the opposite of weak. I'm strong. But now I am feeling weak.

I couldn't come up with one reason for this unthinkable, incredulous news. Frank said immediately without any hesitation while holding my right hand, "I'm with you. We are together. God is with you." All I could do for what appeared to be one of the longest days in my life was stare at Frank. I did and it seemed for nearly an hour.

This journey continued down the road with trips to Elmhurst, Illinois, for Dr. Lawrence Barr visits, blood pressure checks plus meds for three months with no positive improvements.

Pam & Frank

I've never been in this place before. Frank knew this. Frank and I were newlyweds. We dated sixteen months with no trace of illness. Not even a cold. It took me back to when Frank proposed to me at the same restaurant (Lawry's Prime Rib) at the same table (table 20) with the same waitress named Ms. Farmer for our very first date. Now I'm facing what? It's called *congestive heart failure*.

Congestive heart failure, I remember reading, is a condition that affects 5.7 million Americans, according to the US Centers for Disease Control (CDC). It is described as a weakened heart that doesn't pump well and isn't keeping up with the blood supply that the body needs. It causes fatigue, weakness, and shortness of breath. One's heart is no longer able to function properly.

Many people have died from *congestive heart failure*, including people who have excelled in entertainment, business, politics, media, and even sports. They include U.S. presidents John Adams and James Monroe, McDonald's founder Ray Kroc, actress Elizabeth Taylor, jazz singer Lena Horne, and Gospel singer/artist Mahalia Jackson.

Congestive heart failure means that the heart works less efficiently than normal. For a variety of reasons, the heart pumps blood through the heart and body at a slower rate, increasing pressure in the heart. As a result, the heart fails to pump enough oxygen and nutrients to meet the body's needs. The heart chambers stretch to hold more blood to pump through the body. While this may help to keep the blood moving, the heart muscle walls may eventually weaken and become unable to pump as efficiently.

So many get *congestive heart failure* confused with a heart attack that can lead to death. While exercising and eating healthy can reduce the chances of a heart attack, the remedy for a patient like me with *congestive heart failure* is to have a new heart transplant.

I thank God that he gave doctors the power, knowledge, and time to find what was wrong with me and take the right action immediately.

Still, I had to give the news to people I love. Both are forms of heart disease. Congestive heart failure is the result of a weakened heart, but a heart attack occurs when blood is blocked from flowing to the heart.

My sons—Kenneth & John

How can I call my son (John) on his forty-fifth birthday and wish him a happy birthday? It's his Mom. It's Kenneth's Mom. I just received the news. I have congestive heart failure. Say what?

I really thought this over as the paperwork was being processed. A hundred questions ran through my mind. I immediately said a silent prayer. I prayed. I prayed. I prayed. I know, I must be strong. But as earlier indicated, I continued to feel weak.

As moments come and go tracing through my mind, my heart was weak. Damaged. I couldn't honestly let go of what I felt. Where do you go from here? I was reminded of one of Dr. Martin Luther King Jr.'s speeches. Where does *Pam* go from here? I never thought of my life in that wonderful and exciting season that I would have to deal with what's ahead of me on this journey.

As the seconds turned into minutes, into hours, into days, into weeks, and into three months, time passed with the meds. Later, a PICC line is inserted into my left arm to feed me a super drug medication that I later discovered wasn't good for me if I had to have it over six months, plus wearing a life vest, just in case my heart stopped functioning at any given time.

Well, it was less than twenty-one days after the *PICC line* and *life vest* intense meetings with cardiologist specialists Dr. Gene Kim, Dr. Nir Uriel, and Dr. Vallavan Jeevanandam that I walked onto the seventh floor of the University of Chicago Medicine to have the NuPulseCV iVAS balloon pump device implanted in me while I waited for a heart donor.

I did that on July 28, 2016. It was five thirty in the morning. Barely sleeping the night before, I turned to the left of our bed, placing both feet on the floor and stood up without moving for nearly five minutes it seemed, walking slowly to prepare myself for a 5:00 a.m. exit from our home, unsure of the day I would return home.

It took me back to growing up as a very young girl in Saint Albans, West Virginia, and how very special waking up every day was to me. I looked forward to getting up each day in St. Albans, up on the hill, Redd's Hill, getting dressed on this day in my pink cashmere sweater and a faux leather skirt with a pair of black socks and black loafers for school. I wore that same outfit on that same day with two little piggy tails around 7:30 p.m., to Bible class at church on Redds' Hill, sitting on the very front row right in front of Ms. Ophelia. I remember she was a nice, wonderful middle-aged lady. Medium tall with a medium built with a mahogany brown hair. She has small eyes, and Ms. Ophelia wore small square-framed glasses. She never missed a church service. Many years later in July 2016, I was in the University of Chicago Medicine. I need a *new heart.*

July 2016

I was blessed to be in Chicago, which historically has been one of the best cities in getting the best healthcare anywhere in the country. Of the twenty major Chicago hospitals, I was sent to the University of Chicago Medicine, which is located on the South Side on the edge of the University of Chicago campus in Hyde Park. It's about four miles from my home. The University of Chicago Medicine hospital dedicated on Halloween in 1937 consistently ranks among the top facilities in Chicago and the state of Illinois.

Let me tell you, weeks passed, there I was behind the curtain in my room looking at a cotton mock made of 55 percent cotton and 45 percent polyester that has six strings in the back of it with one at the very top and two more located further in the back right above the hips. So what was I supposed to do with that smock? Put it on? I was told to wear it. Not me because every patient was wearing the same kind of cotton smock on same floor (you will read more about the smock later). I knew God, but I could not get any answers.

What happened was, that first day after my 5:30 a.m. arrival to the seventh floor at the University of Chicago Medicine, I was all checked in. I took a seat where the view shows the Chicago downtown skyline with all the high-rise buildings like the Willis Tower, Aon Center, Lake Point Tower, and the Marquette Building. I saw the birthplace of the skyscraper and home to one of the world's greatest iconic skylines, the Hancock Tower with one hundred floors, and then I was called twenty minutes later.

I was walking toward the elevator with Frank, hand in hand, and the guest service ambassador into prep on the fifth floor. I remember it being one of the most challenging times for me with flashbacks of walking into the emergency room in Elmhurst six months earlier. My eyes got teary eyed when she touched the square panel with her right hand, and the door immediately opened; and the three of us walked slowly in with Frank holding my left hand. I squeezed his hand so tight; I remember Frank said, "God's got you and me too!" Tears were still flowing, covering my face.

In a voice that's barely a whisper which is the opposite of my strong but zealous voice heard on my weekly Sunday WVON Radio broadcast, I won't be able to share with listeners, for weeks, or maybe months. I told Frank, "God must order my steps! He's a friend of mine. I know, I can go to god in prayer." I was calling off Gospel song titles like nobody's business.

Somewhere, somehow, someway, the God I've served over the years will see me through. He will order my steps.

See, I never imaged *life* without *my* heart. The *heart* I was born with. I saw me healthy, living my life and doing all the wonderful and exciting events day after day, week after week, and month after month but not so.

Guess what? I found out that your mind can play tricks with you if you're not careful. Mine tried. How do I continue with this?

You know what happened? It was as though not one day slipped empty by. They were full. It was on this particular Sunday morning when my own WVON radio program carried out dynamically by Frank. Frank did what I tried to do every Sunday for listeners near and far.

Can you imagine how I felt? I am the person choosing, selecting encouraging music, giving advice, sharing Mayo Angelo, and Dr. Benjamin May's inspirational quotes, but my role has been switched.

The program uplifted, encouraged, and blessed me. It gave me strength! One Gospel and inspirational song after another! My favorite songs were "He Will See You Through," "Trust Him," "I Know the Lord Will Make a Way," "God Is on Our Side," and "I Know What Prayer Can Do." Wow!

Let me tell you about my husband Frank. I'd start first by saying this blessed, God-fearing, incredible, gifted, intelligent, skilled, impressive, and handsome brown-skinned five-feet, ten inches tall polished gentleman in many ways is *God's* special gift to me. And Frank was there with me every day. I spent a total of *fifty-seven days* in the hospital.

In the *next* chapter, what happened during my second day in the University of Chicago Medicine was very interesting and intriguing. I'm a real *walking miracle*!

Chapter 2

My Journey Begins

University of Chicago Medicine
Day 2
5:00 a.m.

I was connected to the NuPulseCV iVAS balloon pump. Phlebotomist, Mary stepped from behind the pulled curtain rolling a cart. Earlier, a night nurse had awakened me while I slept in a satin multicolored gown to take my vitals. Mary immediately said "Good morning, sunshine" to me just like what nurse Geraldine said with the same greeting the day before.

I wondered if Mary says that to every patient. Am I special to have that lovely greeting? Plus the sun isn't shining through my window. It's 5:00 a.m. "I'm here to draw your blood," she softly said. My questions began with Mary. A needle? I can't stand needles. So I asked, "Are you going to hurt me? What size is the needle? Is it a butterfly needle? How are you this morning?"

Mary smiled while shaking her head side to side as she reached for the butterfly needle. Then with a hand device, she scanned my wristband that was wrapped around my left arm and smiled again. "What do you know about a butterfly needle?" she asked.

I responded, "I know it's thinner." I was holding my breath. I closed my eyes then told Mary not to hurt me. Mary asked me to stretch out my right arm and make a fist. Mary tapped near the elbow bend for a vein pop up that she saw right away and said, "Oh, I see it."

She went about four inches above the vein, reached for the blue smooth stretch tourniquet band and tied it tightly around my arm and wiped the alcohol pad twice as she talked to me very nicely and immediately injected me with the butterfly needle. "Ouch," I said. Mary told me to turn my head to the left and to not think about what she was doing. Seriously?

I remember Mary drawing seven tubes of blood, shaking each tube back-and-forth a couple of times before placing them in her tray on her cart. Mary untied the blue band, slid the needle out of my arm carefully, and then placed a white folded gauze (that's the white cotton surgical dressing) before placing the Band-Aid where she had given me the butterfly needle.

A phlebotomist will do what Mary did today again, tomorrow, and the days that will follow. This reminds me of years ago when I was up on Redd's Hill at home in West Virginia having a conversation with my late aunt Mabel. I miss her. She will always be with me.

I would share with her stories about my two youngsters, John and Kenneth, running in the yard, falling, getting up, falling again, and then on the next fall injuring their right leg and elbow. Both come running into the house with spots of blood dripping, knowing I would give immediate care and attention and fix it but throwing the blame on each other. I'm glad we had Band-Aids. They have colored Band-Aids now.

Mary put a *brown* Band-Aid on me then said, "Have a good day. See you in the morning, same time" and turned to walk toward the drawn curtains to the door for the next patient's room to do the same thing, I think. But will Mary say "Good morning, sunshine" to them too? Guess I will never know.

Leaning back in my bed with my head resting on the pillows that felt so different from my pillows at home, I said to myself, *Self, did Mary say she will see me in the morning same time?* That means she is going to stick me again with another needle! Take seven more tubes of my blood?

Normally, I do not wake up at five o'clock when I'm at home. I'm not used to being awake at this early hour. But I'm in the hospital. I must figure this out. Now and then, I just wonder about being home again. After all, I am in the hospital, schedules change. Didn't they change? Absolutely.

Interesting enough, continuing to lay back in bed, hesitating if I want to get up that early, put my makeup on and my outfit for the day, yes, my makeup, my lipstick, and my outfit on to sit in the chair next to the bed all day while I listen to the inspiring music Frank has playing for me on his Kindle. Frank had said he would arrive early to meet with the doctors.

I positioned myself in bed and began thinking about the blood! Blood songs. Why so much blood being taken from my body in tubes? What's in the blood? Cells carrying *oxygen* throughout one's body, I read.

Lo and behold, it's still early. Peeping from behind the curtain, here's that same nurse from earlier back again for vitals. They just took my vitals two hours ago, and here she is again.

I just set up and let her do her job checking my temperature, blood pressure, and heart rate. The works. I decided not to hold a conversation with her. After all, I needed to be still. No motion during the taking of blood pressure, I'm told.

I glanced up on the wall. The clock is ticking away. Time is passing, and that time won't return. The second hand of the clock was going around and around. It's after 6:00 a.m. I was still waiting for doctors to gather outside my door to enter with the three medical professionals who are in town to check on the NuPulseCV iVAS device that was implanted in me the day before. I waited for them.

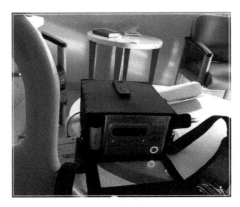

NuPluseCV iVAS

See, in July (2016), I was the *fourth* person in the *world* who was tested, approved, and qualified to have the NuPulseCV iVAS device. There was only three patients who received the device before I got one. Did I say the *first* woman? Yes, the very first woman!

So intriguing, Dr. Vallavan Jeevanandam, chief of cardio surgery, helped design this incredible device with his team. I called him *Dr. J* until I learned how to correctly pronounce his name. He reminded me of Mother Teresa with how he cares for people. Another one of the finest persons I know in the world.

In April 2016, the first patient received this device, I'm told. In July 28, 2016, I was the fourth person being blessed with the NuPulseCV iVAS device. Dr. Jeevanandam, my surgeon, will place the *new heart* in me. I was number 004. Just how blessed can one individual be? Some might say lucky. I choose to say blessed! The NuPulseCV iVAS device is a second heartbeat designed to provide long-term support for those persons with advanced heart failure to assist patients with failing circulation as he or she waits for a heart transplant. I was one of them today!

Dr. Jeevanandam said, "When you're in heart failure, the heart is not generating enough power into the circulation, so you need to increase power."

My story continued like this. I walked on the second day from behind the long drawn, somewhat beige in color curtain out my door, dressed in my black two-piece hooded sweat suit with my string of white pearls around my neck and matching pearl earrings and beige-wedged sandals. I walked the hospital hallways twice. Along with me ticking away was the NuPulseCV iVAS device. It was implanted the day before into my left artery just below my collarbone through a two-inch incision. The batteries and software were inside the external drive. It weighed about six pounds housed in a portable black box.

Walking the Hallways

Everywhere I was, it was there for twenty-seven days in the hallway, in the bed, bathroom visits, morning wash offs sitting in the chair all day and all night. We became friends quickly with the pulsing sound of the device. I thought about the phenomenal, remarkable Gospel singer, preacher, mentor, and retired pastor emeritus of Chicago's Fellowship Baptist Church, the Reverend Dr. Clay Evans recording of "All Night, All Day angels watching over me" and they were watching over me. Angels still, are-watching over me. I am a child of the King!

I am sure you are wondering at this point just how I made it with this device attached to my body for *twenty-seven days*. That's six hundred and forty-eight hours. One day short of four weeks. I knew there were enough prayers going to help me get through, plus I'm a devout Christian. I believe in the higher power. *I believe in God!* I am a child of the King! He's my strength like no other, and I made it! I believe God choose me to be one of His miracles!

My late aunt Mabel sang powerful Gospel songs in her church in St. Albans, West Virginia. She pastored the Apostolic Free Church of God up on Redd's Hill for sixty years. She sang blood songs like "The Blood That Jesus Shed for Me way back on Calvary. The blood that gives me *strength* from day to day, it will never lose its power." Another one she sang was "Oh, the Blood of Jesus/Oh, the Blood of Jesus, it will never lose its power." So many more touching blood songs had blessed me.

In my *next* chapter, I had not anticipated nor imagined what happened over the next three days when I was moved to the corner room suite on the eighth floor at the University of Chicago Medicine. I moved to Room 8011. I couldn't believe it myself.

Chapter 3

My New Device, NuPulseCV iVAS

For the next three days, the sounds of the NuPulseCV iVAS device would resemble a howling cry before I moved to Room 8011. I remember my days longer than a half a dozen Amtrak commuter trains connected together going from Chicago to Washington, DC.

Pam with NuPulseCV iVAS

NuPulseCV iVAS device and me are having a slight problem. Something, it seemed, wasn't exactly right. *Something was wrong.* Dr. Jeevanandam and Coleen arrived in the room and gave the NuPulseCV iVAS device their undivided attention as I looked on.

Here, I was wondering what on earth is happening. After all, we are connected. Colleen (RN) worked closely together with Dr. Jeevanandam, who has incredible bedside manners. Then after a few minutes, I was back as normal in my sweat suit and pearls. NuPulseCV iVAS device was like when it was implanted in me (July 28). I've even received a shoulder bag that fits over my right shoulder to carry the device in. Super!

It's sort of like a backpack, maybe a book bag that was very easy for me to place up on my right shoulder as I move around in my room, walk the hallways, and as it turned out, walked parts of the university campus grounds. After several minutes, I closed my eyes, thinking to myself, the black shaped (as I called it) book bag with a few pockets had brought back memories. It's like the one my grandson, Chris, used for school on Mondays through Fridays. Maybe my granddaughters Sheridan and Chloe have one too.

Then there is more *good news*! See, the room I had earlier seen during one of my hallway walks with one of the nicest male nurses I'd ever met was now my room. I believe his name was nurse Mark.

All I really could do was smile and feel blessed. I was *beaming* with gratefulness and so thankful. We've moved into Room 8011. I walked to my new room by choice. I was asked if I prefer a wheelchair. *No, wheelchair isn't for me.* Not that anything is wrong with a wheelchair but not today. I was moving from Room 8077 in ICU to Room 8011. And I am walking. My new room on Day 3 was one of the coolest, modest, pleasing, and roomiest corner suites ever, like a room maybe in the JW Marriott downtown Chicago or downtown's Ritz Carlton. It was overlooking the city with one view and overlooking DuSable Museum of African American History where I've been dozens of times but not for weeks or months would I return was my other view.

Realizing all the history stored and viewed across the street, I could not cross the street and visit the museum that became an educational resource for African American history and culture. An institution that opened in 1961. Again, I couldn't walk across the street and visit.

I couldn't ride the giant, huge vertical revolving Ferris wheel in Navy Pier. It's one of Chicago skyline staples that stands about two hundred feet tall with forty-two swanky high-tech gondolas that can hold up to ten passengers or just maybe ride the musical carousel that features thirty-six hand-painted animals (more of my speed). Anyway, there were only four corner suites in the hospital. I had been blessed with one!

God blessed me for *twenty-seven days* with the corner suite! I'm reminded of Gospel artists Evelyn Turrentine Agee's song "God Did It" and the Georgia Mass Choir song "He Keeps on Proving Himself Over and Over Again!" These two songs grabbed me by the ankles. I was singing away! Whew! I held family meetings and my son Kenneth's birthday cake in a rather small party/gathering. Mai from Nail Pro with her beautiful daughter groomed my nails. I held court with family visitors and very close family friends.

I was really surrounded by a relatively large circle of family and friends. What a wonderful, marvelous feeling to have family and friend visits. I marvel how blessed I am because I understand people have schedules, events, responsibilities, everyday jobs, and take time to come to the University of Chicago to visit with me. Wow!

My Room 8011

There was a long brown couch, three tables and several chairs, a tall oblong closet that held my wardrobe of slacks, and multiple colored blouses that I changed into each day after describing in detail for Frank to deliver from home. I practically could hardly wait to set up my (seven) photos that Frank had taken off the kitchen wall at home for me. Framed photos of family and family friends. Family photos all around me.

I placed Frank's Kindle with inspiring music that repeatedly made me feel confident about myself. Music was playing all day and night between the photos. *There was really no end to the inspiring songs that surrounded me day in and day out.* I remember positioning my three beige battery-operated candles on the mantle. So that's that.

Oh, nurses, at times, were confused with my three candles that brightly shined during the night. The candles reminded me of hope during one of the most challenging times in my life. It was a delightful feeling in my home away from home, not knowing it was going to be like that for nearly four weeks. Surprising me, Frank popped up from behind. The curtain was bearing two dozen gorgeous long-stemmed *red* roses in his left arm. They were red as L'Oreal and Rihanna's Fenty Beauty lipstick. Red as Red Hot tamales. Red as the red cherry tomatoes I had sliced in half and carefully placed in his romaine salad I fixed before leaving our home in late July. Later, floral dish plants, get-well-soon and thinking-of-you cards began to arrive.

So many people I love and cared about *didn't know where I was* or even know my *real* health condition; however, *some knew.* I honestly admit I was in a place of trying to deal with an illness that nearly took my breath completely away. How do you tell that? Obviously, my condition was not the news you want to broadcast. I'm a broadcaster too. Family members agreed. I was under doctors' care and appreciate the prayers when conversations arise about Pam. That's the message.

My decision was when I wanted to talk, I would. See, I had previously told Broadcast Ministers Alliance (BMA) host Archbishop Hall during the July 21 telecast taping that I would be away under doctors' care indefinitely but had looked forward to returning. Sure enough, on October 6, 2016, of Broadcast Ministers Alliance's telecast taping, I returned as cohost with host Archbishop Lucius Hall, he prayed for me everyday.

Frank would sit in for me on my Sunday WVON radio program and share same message the family agreed on as well as represented at several dozen engagements in my absence. I remember Frank going across the street from where I was to DuSable Museum of African American History to represent me at Bishop Gordon's special event. He turned around and waved at me after crossing the street as he walked into the museum doors. I waved back. What else could I do?

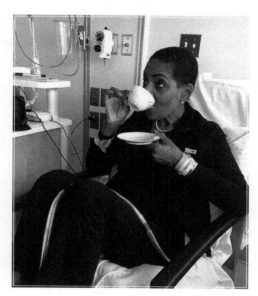

Water in my Tea Cup

My wonderful dear sister Valoria visited me bearing gifts—a lovely greeting card, a placemat she made for me, and a very special China saucer and teacup. (She knew my love for tea every day.) Valoria wrote this in my journal:

> What can I say to a woman of faith? One who's been walking and not just talking faith but who lives by faith. Stand and continue to stand on God's Word. You know that his Word is true! God is great and greatly to be raised. He will do all things well! Stand strong and hold on. Your Better is coming! There's a miracle with your name on it. Our God is a miracle-working God!

A dear friend who had read as far as this as far as I had written said, "Tell you story. Tell it." And I didn't know that another one of my dearest friends, Beverly, would take the train from Palatine to downtown Chicago's Ogilvie Transportation Center to visit me. Nearly thirty-five miles from Palatine, the trip would take forty-five minutes to Chicago. Frank picked her up.

Beverly's early afternoon visit on Monday, August 1, in Room 8011 was so pleasant and enjoyable. She came bearing gifts. I had heard the door open. When Beverly peeped from behind the curtain looking beautiful as always, she said to me, "You look beautiful!"

We hugged. Then we hugged again. Then I got teary-eyed on the third hug. We held on to each other with Frank standing close by. Seconds later, I, along with my attached friend (NuPulseCV iVAS device), sat down in my rather long beige chair. I told Beverly in one breath, "Sit down. I'm sorry" speaking of the sound from my device.

I explained the NuPulseCV iVas to Beverly. The pump kept working improving my circulation while giving my heart a rest. Oh, yes! I thank God! Beverly bowed her head and put her face very close to mine. *We prayed. Then we cried.* Beverly's visit lasted nearly an hour before leaving to catch the three twenty-five Metra train returning to her home.

Our friendship boasts with many qualities because we finish each other's sentences, laugh at silly jokes, laugh at each other, and lean on each other when our strengths seems to give out. I remember when Beverly and I shopped one day at Stein Mart, DSW, Hobby Lobby, TJ Maxx and Marshall's. Before leaving, Beverly wrote in my journal:

> You are always thinking of others. The day you went into the hospital, I received a card and your signature trademark...a tea bag.
>
> I love you girl and praying God's power of health, strength, and recovery for you. You are very special to me. Love you much and Stein Mart, here we you get better.

I remember Beverly turning to me before going behind the curtain saying, "Pam, hang in there. I love you!" Oh, how I enjoyed her visit. I know, friends are special. I know a friend is someone you love and who loves you. They respect you, and you respect them. Someone whom you can trust and who trusts you. A friend is honest. That's Bev. I have more too! Close friends, that is. Then I look out the window over at DuSable Museum of African American History just wishing I could visit. So close but not possible.

Finally at the very end of the day on Monday, August 3, after Beverly, Daphine, Helen, Valoria, Douglas, Darryl, my doctors' visit, and nurses taking vitals, blood draw, eating breakfast, lunch, and dinner, Frank prepared to depart. We held hands, we looked into each other's eyes; and then we prayed together, and we hugged.

I asked the question, "When do you think the heart will come? When, babe? How long am I going to be here?"

Frank said, "It's in God's hands. Be patient, Pam. Be patient."

Once upon a time, I had lot of patience. But in this situation, my patience wore thin, at times. My life was at stake. We really didn't say much to each other. After that then, I reached for another hug.

In my *next* chapter, what happened on the fifth day had me, Frank, and three more dear family friends in tears, all of us together.

Chapter 4

A False Alarm

Day 5
August 4, 2016

Early morning forecast: a beautiful day was expected, super-hot, and one should limit their time outside because it will feel like one hundred degrees. Rain about midnight.

After reading another page in *One-Minute Prayers for Women* and *God's Promises for Your Every Need* (two very special gifts from my neighbor with the same name and initials as mine), getting early morning vitals, having blood draw, dressed, ordering, and then eating breakfast and having prayer, I was walking down the hallways with Frank as we held each other's hands. The question remains on my mind that I asked in the last chapter was, "When will I get my *new heart?* How long will I be here?" I know that I believe that eventually, the heart will come for me. And I prayed I will return home.

Nurse Ola entered my room with a smile. It seemed as wide as a rainbow that appeared after a Chicago rainstorm. I really admired Nurse Ola.

One day, I was walking out of a nearby Staples office supply store. I had purchased a package of Pilot C-2 very fine, super smooth, comfortable, and refillable writing pens and one package of LC-61 Series Brother ink cartridges.

I remember seeing a *double* rainbow in the *sky when I walked out of Staples.* Yes, a *double rainbow.* It was breathtaking to view. I just stood there in admiration. I remember reading one day, "According to the art and philosophy of Feng Shui, that *double rain*bows are considered symbolic of transformation in your *life.* The material world is represented by the first rainbow while the second rainbow is the spiritual world." Wow!

From the first time I met Nurse Ola, he remained kind, informative, caring, and telling me to *be patient* and your *heart* is coming." He reminded me of Frank so much. He's caring, encouraging, and kind. He has a quiet voice. Nurse Ola only worked the night shift, I'm told. I looked forward to his calm presence in my room every night.

As the days came and went, I was delighted by shared conversations from more visitors as they passed through with smiles, cards, good wishes, and loving messages. They were, of course, so surprised to see me sitting up in the chair in the left corner of my room fully dressed with make up on right next to the bed with my white-and-black music blanket thrown over the bed and some very inspiring music playing. My neighbor Pam wrote in my journal that my neighbor Pat had given me:

> God is good. When I moved on Michigan Avenue and Pat introduced us, we have been good friends ever since. We have the same name, initials, and we got married within months of each other. You are a woman of God. God loves you and so do I.

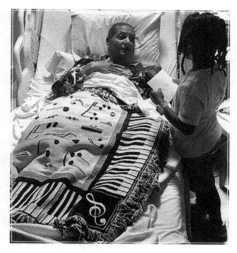

Chloe speaks to me under my music blanket

It was still Day 5. I was wearing black dress slacks, black casual cotton camisole tank top, and white-and-red long high-collared 100 percent polyester Michael Kors blouse with cuffed sleeves saying "Hello."

The NuPulseCV iVAS device was pumping. We were very connected as we waited for those words that several nurses had told me will come, they say. Meanwhile, my device kept pumping, pumping away. I think if I knew how to croquet, my hands would be busy shaping yards of thread into a beautiful shawl for my daughter, John's wife. Her name is Andrea. She's amazing in so many ways.

The *heart transplant team* at the University of Chicago Medicine consisted of many persons. "They will call you or show up in your room with the news that I'm waiting for," it was said to me.

Once that occurs, I will be so *happy*! I will be so *very happy*. Excited. I want to *live*! I want to live a healthy and normal life! But I need *a heart*. See, the *heart* is a muscle that is a little bigger than the size of your fist located in the middle of your chest at the center of your rib cage. A pump that moves blood through-out your body. And I have a *diseased* heart.

So later that afternoon, peeping behind the curtain, three of my dear sister friends arrived. I was so glad to see them—Sheryl, Carol, and Pat! I didn't hear the door open either.

We often have get-togethers for *girls' night out* to see a movie or stage play. We have even taken turns visiting each other's home, having interesting conversations about current events, and eating some real tasty food. We were now laughing, sharing conversation, and talking about my attire and my cultured pearl necklace set. Then the telephone rang. I remember being nervous to answer. "Is this the news I've been waiting for?"

It was cardiologist Dr. Sarswat, saying, "Pam, congratulations! You have a heart!"

I said, "A *heart*?"

She replied, "Yes! A heart! Your blood will be drawn shortly."

As Dr. Sarswat was speaking, one of the team doctors rushed quickly into my room, pulled the curtain back, began wiping my right arm down with an alcohol swab where the elbow bends, tied the blue band on my arm, and drew blood in several tubes.

Oh, did I say I had to get up on the bed quickly to remove my blouse off on the right arm? I was too excited to ask if it was a butterfly needle or even say that I had had blood drawn earlier that morning. I was quiet. Real quiet. I didn't imagine this happening. She hurriedly rushed out of the room with the drawn tubes of blood. I was so excited that I'm not sure exactly what I said. In the moment into the moments following, prep was taking place. Of course, getting ready was okay.

My iPhone was ringing. The volume was really high. I turned right to reach over on the table next to my bed and answered. It's Dr. Jeevanandam, my transplant surgeon. He's on a plane saying *congratulations* to me and that he wanted to be there when the *heart* would come for the heart surgery. Dr. Jeevanandam was leaving town on the plane in his seat, preparing to take off and returning the next day, I believe.

He stated, "Dr. Ota would be doing the surgery tonight." I was happy. I was sad. I said to myself, *How could this be? How can I be happy and sad?* I said to myself, *How could this be? How can I be happy and sad?*

The point is, Dr. Jeevanandam was the doctor I believed would take out my damaged heart and sew the new heart in. Dr. Jeevanandam was headed out of state. He was on a plane. I didn't even know if he really returned the next day.

Anyway, I called Frank on my cell after Dr. Jeevanandam hung up. Frank was speechless for a few seconds. I said eight words, "Babe, I have a heart! Surgery is tonight!" I was ecstatic! I was thrilled. I was on cloud nine! "Frank, did you hear me?"

Frank had been running errands and returning with my dinner request—jerk chicken, cabbage, rice and beans, and plantains. Frank finally said, "Yes, I heard you. I'm on my way." I wondered what was going through Frank's head at that moment.

It's been five days in the hospital and with the hospital food services that I wasn't used too. *It was different.* The doctors had called in to say I could not eat certain items from the menu placed next to me on top of my nightstand. Now I loved the bananas, cold milk with whole grain cheerios, popsicles, and broiled eggs. That was about it.

For me, I was craving some of Frank's home-cooked meals, especially some of his baked chicken with sweet chili sauce and roasted sweet potatoes. Maybe Millers' Pub Lemon Chicken from downtown on Wabash or a Caesar salad from Pockets in Hyde Park. Pam (the patient) and the hospital food service, well, I suppose, needed to adjust, one might say. We were not getting alone.

I was waiting for the next steps. I was crying like a baby. Crying like a newborn baby, okay. Tears burst forth like water from a dam, spilling down my face. I believe *we all had tears in our eyes*. We all had tears in our eyes. Frank arrived and greeted all of us. We hugged and hugged again. I didn't want to let go of Frank. I held on so tight. Tears were still flowing.

Frank listened as all four of us give him minute by minute what just happened. He looked on in amazement. Then my cellphone rang; it's Colleen. Remember RN Colleen? (She worked with Dr. Jeevanandam). I called her Dr. Jeevanandam's assistant.

"Pam," she said in a very low soft voice, "it's Colleen. *False alarm*. Everything isn't matching up. I'm so sorry. We will keep waiting. I'll see you tomorrow, okay?" That was it. That was it. It was like my heart dropped to the floor. What was I to say?

Now, now, a *false alarm*? It's a warning given about something that failed to happen. It didn't happen August 4. It didn't happen. Pointless to say, I was speechless. I couldn't say one single word. Nothing!

Dropping my head in disappointment because something didn't add up with the new heart for me to receive. Was it the blood? What does one do? What does one think? We prayed. It calmed me greatly. I was reminded of the Gospel song by artist Jessy Dixon "I Know What Prayer Can Do."

Two days later, on Saturday evening, there was still no new news about a *heart*, more wonderful family and gracious friend's visits. My youngest son, Kenneth, has arrived from Richmond, Virginia, with my granddaughter Chloe.

Two of my goddaughters were also in town. Kedra is from Atlanta, Georgia, and Cynthia is from Orlando, Florida.

We have celebrated my son Kenneth's forty-third's birthday. Cynthia's birthday too. Cynthia wrote in my journal:

> Mother, Friend, Forever Boss, knowing you for the bulk of my life for over thirty-five years! You have been there for every major event in my life! I can't explain in words how important you are to me! I have watched God's favor surround you! It's been a blessing to watch God bless you and then watch you bless others! I'm so glad to be here. You look beautiful! I can't wait to see what God has in store for you! I'll always be here when you need me!

It's August 6 in Room 8011 with a delicious two-layered tasty caramel cake that Daphine brought for the party with slices left over and an edible arrangement. So Good! Dear family sister and friend Adrienne visited and wrote in my journal:

"My dear sister, I love you more and more each day. The world knows you, but I know you the best way! The *true friend*, sister, woman of God and God's will be done in your life!"

It's my son Kenneth's birthday. Kenneth is my youngest son. I remember introducing Kenneth to one of the nurses as my son in from Richmond, and behold, it seemed Kenneth was in charge as if he had personally carried me for nine months in the womb and had given birth to me. But I knew he was concerned about his mom. Both John and Kenneth were.

Next in Chapter 5, we waited for more *heart news*. You can't guess who visited me with a beautiful bunch of flowers on Day 12. I was so touched.

Chapter 5

Gospel Music as Medicine

Day 11
Sunday, August 7

At 4:30 a.m. and after several in-depth discussions with Dr. Jeevanandam, I now know I will not leave the University of Chicago Medicine to *host* my WVON Live *Gospel with Pam Morris-Walton* program for *weeks*.

On the previous Sunday, I had listened to the program and thought the *next* Sunday I could be in live on WVON. Leaving was completely out of the question.

I had been in the habit of leaving from the 8:00 a.m. Apostolic Faith Church morning worship service about twelve blocks from home then returning home to pick up my laptop and a number of Gospel cd's, and then drive down the Dan Ryan Expressway to Exit 61B to turn left on 87th Street to WVON Radio station.

When I traveled on the Dan Ryan Expressway, I felt safe. I felt good. That's a freeway in the City of Chicago that runs from the Circle Interchange with 1-290 near downtown Chicago through the South Side of the City of Chicago. The freeway was named for Dan Ryan Jr., a former president of the Cook Country Board of Commissioners.

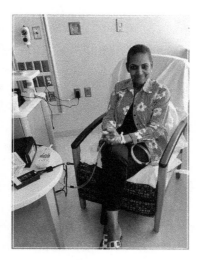

I'm dressed going nowhere

So here I am, Pam, sitting in the chair dressed and thinking, What I have given *with all my heart* every Sunday to countless listeners from across the United States of America, whether listening online, iheart radio live on 1690 AM will be given to me *indefinitely*.

One Sunday, a listener, enjoying her vacation in Hawaii lying on the beach called into my program, thanking me for the inspiring and uplifting music that was making her day, and she made her song request. I played her song and felt her smiling from miles away.

I didn't know then that's *twenty-four hours* of music over eight weeks that I was away would happen; however, I was still blessed. See, it was music, *good music* designed to encourage, uplift, and brighten one's day and week. Wow! And I love radio! There really is no end to this art form of music. *Music* is a universal language. "Gospel music," I call it as the late professor Thomas Andrew Dorsey called it "good news music."

One thing I know for certain, music does affect our daily lives. Music affects our emotions. When one listens to happy music, one feels happier. Upbeat songs with energetic rhythms tend to make one excited and all pumped up. Personally speaking, *I love Gospel music!* Who would have ever thought? I looked forward after 8 a.m. Sunday worship service to my WVON Gospel Broadcast. But not this Sunday, not even the next Sunday, and those weeks were difficult to accept.

Listen, the truth is, I didn't know how long my stay in the University of Chicago Medicine would be. Not what it turned out to be. Three days short of two months. Yes, nearly two months. See, after never being sick before beyond a cold or flu like symptoms in my life, this medical condition threw me for a loop larger than the downtown Chicago Loop filled with over twenty-five hundred fine shops and restaurants. A devoted wife to Frank, professional talk show cohost, a strong-willed woman of God, and in the University of Chicago Medicine waiting for a new heart—the right heart—whenever it may come.

So now I continue to listen to Frank host my three-hour hot Gospel radio program on WVON. It made me feel much better. I remember getting teary-eyed as I continued to listen to the incredible moving music.

Frank arrived in my room around three in the afternoon with dinner. Yes! Yes! Yes! The food went right into my mouth. I ate every bit of that Jerk chicken, dirty rice, cabbage, and yams. The food was delicious.

After eating every ounce of food, I threw my plate in the nearby trash container and wiped my mouth with the back of my hand and immediately shared conversation with Frank about the outstanding radio program he hosted on my behalf.

Of course, speaking of food, I would have like to go to one of our favorite restaurants downtown Chicago, so I could order grilled garlic shrimp with garlic butter and baked potato with sour cream and chives. Oh, well, wishful thinking, My Pastor, Dr. Smith, MD, and wife, Susan, blessed me with another lovely and encouraging visit and a very special prayer. And there were other guests that graced me with their presence and prayers.

Godson Jermaine visits and wrote in the journal:

"God has been good to you and continues to be with you each and every moment. God still heals and is going to heal you. In the words of the Gospel songwriter, "Don't give up on God because He won't give up on you."

The very next day, I was sitting with the NuPulseCV iVAS device sounds just sounding away. I stood up to look out my window.

This time, I was looking to my left not that far away. I saw a helicopter landing on top of another adjoined hospital building. A patient on a stretcher was met by a team of people I suppose were nurses and doctors. I couldn't tell.

I soon learned that persons had come to the University of Chicago Medicine from everywhere around the country for healthcare. I was here for a *heart*.

I turned to sit back in beige very comfortable beige chair filled with several pillows to read from pages in the *Daily Word* when peeping from around the curtain is this lovely, beautiful lady with gorgeous features and long brownish black hair. I didn't hear the door open. *It's Shelia.* I tried to step over to hug her. She met me half the way, reaching her right hand toward me, presenting me with a lovely bouquet of colorful flowers. They were so beautiful. So pretty. Absolutely attractive like her. We hugged.

Sheila sat down, and nothing else in the world mattered right now. All that mattered were these moments we had together with the nicest conversation ever coming from her *heart*. Shelia looked right in my eyes. Shelia held my hand. Shelia then said to me, "You are in God's hands, and my husband will make sure you get the right heart!"

Believe me, I didn't know what to say after Shelia said those words. So we looked at each other and smiled. I clearly remember what had taken place days before with the *false alarm*. Did the donor's heart fail before it could be retrieved? Why was the transplant called off? Was it the right size? Was the blood an exact match? I didn't know.

I looked out the window where the sun was shining bright, and it felt good. Real good! Did I mention that Shelia is Dr. Jeevanandam's lovely wife? Out of all the people in the world, Shelia *could* have visited. She had taken the time to visit me. I will tell you now Shelia's visit made me feel so special. A humbling and warm experience!

And for your information, Shelia's conversation continued about my condition and the actual heart transplant. She knew what I was going through and going to go through. She encouraged me.

Maybe because, well, hours after Shelia's visit, I thought back about my wait for the heart. After tests and I mean many, many tests were completed and my case discussed at the morning transplant meeting, Dr. Kim had telephoned me at home to share the news. And having had the NuPulseCV iVAS device implanted in me on July 28, I moved up on the list to 1A for *a heart* because of my condition.

Well, I found out waiting for the donor really can be *tedious*, *exhausting*, and *very, very tiresome*. It could be several *months* or *several years*. That's saying a lot. Did I say several months, several years? How can one maintain a life? It would change your life. See, the blood type must be compatible and also the body size of the donor's heart. In my case, with my high-risk condi-

44

tion, I remained in the hospital for *a heart* with my implanted device under a month.

"God really smiled on me!" The gifted Gospel singer out of Gary, Indiana, Pharis Evans sang a song "Thank You" that came all over me. I kept humming it.

Late afternoon, the door opened. Behind the curtain was Frank with the renowned, awesome Fellowship Missionary Baptist Church founder Pastor Emeritus *Rev. Dr. Clay Evans.* I was smiling. We hugged. We sang hymns. We prayed together. Reverend Evans stood up and said, "I'm ready to go. I didn't come to stay long!" He prepared to walk to the door behind the curtain to the elevator with Frank when several nurses stopped him to introduce themselves and share conversation. They loved his music and preaching. What an awesome blessing! It was so uplifting.

Then from Atlanta, Georgia, my uncle Beauford with his wife, Yvonne, appeared from behind the curtain. We hugged. We talked. Beauford had walked the hospital hallways with me before heading to Shaw's Crab House on Hubbard Street for dinner. Didn't I want to go too? One of my favorite restaurants too.

My uncle Beauford is two months older than I am. He's tall. Handsome. Smart. A great guy.

I remember the good old days back in school in Saint Albans, West Virginia! It was a period (of time) in my past that I thought was so great and better than the present time. Everything seemed to make sense and was possible. It took several of my aunts getting together and their sister, my mom (Paskalena), to gather around the kitchen table and talk from lunch to supper-time about the good old days. Days, for instance, when we just had good times, it seemed all the time, one day after the other. We had some real cool childhood experiences.

Pastor Monica, my family friend, drove from Milwaukee, Wisconsin, the night before I went into the hospital to take me to dinner on Wednesday, July 27. We went to Riva's at Navy Pier. I ordered fried shrimp, baked potato with butter, sour cream, and chives and a side order of spinach. I sure did eat all my food, okay. We hugged. Pastor Monica reached for my hands and prayed for me before returning to her home in Milwaukee that very same night. What a friend!

The rest of the day went by with more pleasant and encouraging visits, demonstrating so much love from Dr. Terry Mason, Patrick, Joe, Pat and Russell, John and Andrea, Mary Ann, Rhonda, Tecora, Vanessa, Daphine, Lionel and Etta, and Douglas! Dr. Smith and Susan returned. God really blessed me with some incredible family friends!

Daphine wrote (again) in my journal and this time said:

> It's such a blessing to watch God move on your behalf. I thank God for you! I love you! I know faith and prayer works! I have so much more to say, but my heart is filled with nothing but love and respect for you. Thanks for allowing me to be a part of your life.

Much later, Frank was sitting with me on the couch. We were holding hands and sharing conversation about how God has been so *good* to us during this waiting process for *a heart*. We shared places we love and museums we yet need to revisit and our next trip. I told Frank about the tests scheduled at 8:00 a.m. the next day. I was, of course, not smiling.

The nurse will bring the cotton smock (the cotton smock that tied three places in the back right above the hips) into my room for me to put on as I waited for the individual with the stretcher to arrive to put me on with my device and take me for my test. I mean, I mean, I really didn't care for the smock. But it's *required* to wear with no jewelry, no makeup, and no perfume when going for tests and surgeries.

See, what I remember most about the cotton smock was if you must lean forward, just be careful. Oh, well. Frank tried to make me feel better about wearing it. Job well done. I must give credit to Frank.

In Chapter 6, Dr. Uriel looked directly in my face and answered my question with two words. He's very direct. He's *no-nonsense*. Then that same day in the evening, I cried again. Maybe worse than a baby's cry. I screamed. I believed I yelled and cried again. Why?

Chapter 6

I Can't Believe I'm Still Here

Day 18
August 14

It's the beginning of the third week. I was up with no makeup on. I was sitting in the chair next to the bed in my sleeping gown. It's six in the morning. I was sending *good morning* text messages to some family and close family friends around the country. I was thinking, *They can give me a break with my blood draws? Really, Pam?* My morning vitals and meds were completed.

I've remained prayerful on this journey. The song "I Know What Prayer Can Do" was on my lips. I was singing to myself. Next, I sang "It's All in His Hands."

A little later, I was revisiting every card and reading each message. They were positioned so lovely in my room. I was doing all I can one week and a half in the hospital to stay strong.

Today so far, it has been 132 hours waiting for *a heart. Will it come? When?*

I couldn't believe I was still here. I've never stayed in any *one place* this long before in my life. True enough, I was yet holding on, and it's not easy for me at all.

Anyway, I sensed another nurse will be entering my room any moment with the cotton smock I requested earlier for me to put on for my scheduled *cardiopulmonary stress test*. It's now almost 8:00 a.m. The test is highly sensitive, non-invasive, and the exercise stresses your body's systems by making them work faster and harder.

Here I was, wondering what's going to happen. Will I have good test results? I was believing, I will. *I believe in God!*

Then Frank called for our morning prayer and asked how I was doing. "Just okay," I said. It was very necessary. I felt to share with him that I couldn't get to sleep last night. One eye open, one eye closed. Was it because of the false alarm ten days ago? Was it because I kept thinking about how many days am I going to be here? The visitors that came and left? Was it the next test I needed to have superior results from?

So many questions traveled through my mind. Why did this happen to me? Why Pam? What went wrong to cause this?

I ended up nodding off to sleep while viewing the video of artists Richard Smallwood's live in Atlanta Recording of "Total Praise!" That inspiring video blessed me. I remember watching it repeatedly.

Next day, Dr. Uriel came in the room with his team with the biggest smile on his face. The team of doctor's steps back. He stayed forward and reached his arms out for a hug. He then sat. He started talking immediately about my test results which included the *cardiopulmonary stress test*. I rode that bicycle with all I had during my test. I really did, like I was riding the bike path at 31st Street Harbor Street Beach on the South Side of Chicago.

That test was also checking my heart rate while the EKG was being monitored with the amount of oxygen I was breathing. Also, it was being measured too. Dr. Uriel looked at me straight in the eyes and said, "You're doing great!" He repeated, "Great! Real great!"

Realizing that was the opposite of what he had said weeks ago when he looked me in the eyes and said with much force, "Do you want to live?"

I answered, "Yes!"

Then he said, "You need a heart! Not a pacemaker, not a stent but a heart!"

Frank was there then. He's looking quite shocked. Speechless. I couldn't help but say, "Yes, sir."

Then I said, "I can't stand needles!"

Well, Dr. Uriel said, "Get use to them! Lots of them." And was he ever so right? Absolutely, I had lots of them!

Dr. Uriel's visit was longer than I expected. Nice. The doctors and their team were very knowledgeable of my faith and belief in God. I had told them, "I know God works miracles. He is a healer. He has never failed me yet. Again, he has never failed me yet."

So Dr. Uriel began to ask me about the church I attend. I had been streaming the Sunday morning worship services at 8:00 a.m. every Sunday while in the hospital but not today. I had tests. Dr. Uriel was there.

I told Dr. Uriel he had to meet my amazing pastor, Dr. Horace E. Smith, MD. I Invited him to come visit one Sunday in our worship service. "He agreed," he said.

After the good report given to me, I said, "Dr. Uriel, I have a question."

He said, "Okay."

I said, "Dr. Uriel, what's next?"

Immediately, he said two words before leaving, "A heart!"

At that point, all I could do was look into Dr. Uriel's eyes and said, "I'm waiting. Thank you, Dr Uriel." It was then that

I felt I'd better hush. I did. Not another word flowed from out of my mouth.

After Dr. Uriel turned from me and left, Nurse Katie stepped into my room. She's a loving, kind, attentive, and caring nurse every time.

Of course, I did mention earlier that there were meds every day. Meds were taken with cranberry and orange juice. Not water. I know; I know that's not normal. I will explain (in the *next* chapter).

Pastors Angela and Roderick, also Sharon, Shante, Yvonne, Tyler, Andrea, and Daphine, along with my sonsJohn and Kenneth, visited me with touching prayers, laughs, and floral arrangements—an edible arrangements filled with pineapple daisies, cantaloupe wedges, grapes, and strawberries. I had some fried chicken wings. Yummy! I received another teddy bear. That made three teddy bears. I was feeling quite special. You should have seen that room.

My son's wife, Andrea, wrote in my journal:

"Mom, you are strong and mighty in spirit. God's hands continue to surround you, hold you, and comfort you. His favor is upon you as it always been upon you. Keep fighting and praying; God s with you through it *all*.""

Then later, Frank, also Daphine, experienced some moments that had me in *tears*. I screamed. I yelled so loud that my voice had to be heard down the hospital halls. I saw a side of me I had never seen before coming out of me. It was awful.

What happened was, you are given a needle when they put the IV in your arm. It changes every three days. The left arm is the best arm since the daily blood draw is usually done from the right arm.

Well, my rolling veins kept rolling that Sunday late evening, so every time I was stuck by the nurse practitioner Jason whose called the best nurse on the floor to give you the needle, that nurse could get it in my arm with *no problem*. He began with the ultrasound that showed the veins position and movement, then he proceeded. First try, no luck. I begin to *cry*. Second try, no luck. I *cried* some more. It was so painful. The third try, I hollered, I screamed, and I kept crying. That was it. I hollered loud, "Stop it. Stop it now!" The screaming stopped. It wasn't good moments for anyone to experience or even speak of. He then stopped trying. He gave up.

That Sunday on August 14 around 6:00 p.m., I called it quits! I couldn't take the excruciating pain! You don't hurt, Pam. *I had reached my breaking point. I had had enough. Enough.* In fact, I wanted to give up the wait for a new heart. I had experienced some ugly moments not describable on this page.

I remember so well that Frank was asking everyone to leave the room. That meant the nurses—and Daphine who tried to never miss a day to visit me. It was just me and Frank. I was sitting in the chair, and if I remember correctly, I was not being really nice a bit. I was *boohooing* something awful.

Frank came over toward me and stepped over both of my legs. You heard me right. Frank stepped over both of my legs, staring in my face and grasping my hands, saying, "I wish I could take the needles for you. You have to hold on! You have to. *I'm not going to lose you.* It's going to be all right. Breathe. God's got you! I love you."

I took a deep breath. It got better when I looked up at Frank's face, letting go of his hands, and wiping tears away as they drip down my face. I calmed down slowly.

The nurse now on duty came to take my vitals. She immediately looked over at the candles. I had three of them positioned between get-well cards and thinking-of-you cards, plants, and framed family photos. It was so lovely sight to see.

Oh, each candle had the look of a real flame. They even flicker like a real candle. However, it's a LED wax candle, battery operated. The nurse began to raise her voice to say, "You can't have those in your room." I just looked at her. Then I said smiling, "You can blow them out." By then she realized the candles were not real. Funny!

All I can say now was "Good night!" What a day.

Inside the fourth week in Chapter 7 what was the news and why can't I take meds with water. Water is pure, a transparent, tasteless chemical substance that is the main constituent of earth's streams, lakes, and oceans. Healthy. Good.

Chapter 7

All in the Family

Day 25
August 21

As you continue to read my story, you must remember *twenty-five*. Important. Very important! Very, very important! The sun beams were cutting through my window. I sat wishing I was on the beach in Miami, Florida, with our scheduled trip, relaxing in the sunny beautiful weather; and you know by now I cannot host my WVON radio show either.

I told Frank to expect my call in from me. After all, the message we agreed for everyone was, "I'm away under doctors' care. Thank you for your prayers, right?" Right. Guess what? I'm still away. But the other thing every day on my mind is *a new heart.*

Will it happen today? Tomorrow? The next day? Or next one? Maybe the next one. I'm up dressed in my white 100 percent cotton blouse that has illustrations all over from beginning to end showcasing the words Paris, France, Seattle, New York, San Francisco, Rome—places I had been before; and I would love to travel there again.

I was sitting next to the bed in the chair doing my morning selfie photos (again) to send out to my family and goddaughters when the nurse on duty comes into my room with my morning meds. Every morning seems to be the same. Meds. Meds. Meds.

I asked for juice. We carried on a brief conversation after returning with cranberry and orange juice. She told me, "I like your room."

I responded, "Well, thank you."

She further said to me, "There's a lot of love in this room."

I smiled and said, "You are right. It is!" She stood there admiring and staring at the long-stemmed red roses that now have bloomed out; and really, they don't look for real at all, but they are real. She looked at all the greeting cards, the plants, and told me again, "There's a lot of love in this room."

I responded, "Yes, you are right. Lots of love!"

Frank hadn't arrived yet. He's still on WVON—sounding real good! I texted him. Frank texted me right back. Then I waited for the right time to call in to speak over the airwaves with greetings to our listeners. It's Frank's fourth broadcast, sitting at the microphone for me. Wow! What a guy! Colleen (RN) came into the room, smiling and saying hello in the brightest way then sharing certain kind of *exercises* I needed to perform.

First moving my leg up and down within a certain time limit. I did well. I moved those legs of mine up and down, up and down. Second walking the hallway back and forth within a certain time limit. I did well twice. We chatted. Colleen left the room after a brief conversation and the finished exercises with a smile.

Later, Tecora returned (another dear family friend) and came from behind the curtain. Sharp as one can be, smiling. I smiled back at her.

In the middle of our conversation, I interrupted Tecora. I asked if she would sing me a song and guess what? She did. Right then. Right there. Tecora sang CeCe Winans's inspiring song "Alabaster Box." It was so beautiful and reminded me of sitting at one of the front tables for a forty-five-minute set at the Promontory in Hyde Park months ago where she had sung. Friends are special. Priceless. A gift!

More family and family friends visited me. Penny and Johnny, Joe, Yvonne and Tyler, Patrick, Carey and Cindy, and Charles. Valoria, Chaga, and Althea did too.

Althea wrote in the journal:

> As usual, but especially right now, today, you are beautiful. A sight for sore eyes. We are so happy to see you and see you looking and living so well. We never before seen someone look so well in a place like this. Beautiful. Amazing. Inspiring. Powerful. Purposeful. Nice to see you being your wonderful, magnificent, loving, and adorable self. Continue on. We love you so much.

I don't know how to put it. I just shared with Frank. How good it felt as I waited for *a heart* to have gracious, loving family and family friends. It just felt good! *I value friendships.*

Members of my family

It's Monday. August 22, 2016. 6:30 a.m.

I wrote in my journal:

> Tracy from abc7chicago have given a gor-
> geous weather forecast. The sun rays are
> bright, cutting through the window. I wait
> for the next step. I'm in the hospital at the
> University of Chicago Medicine. But my
> real thoughts are elsewhere like shopping
> or just browsing around at Stein Mart, TJ
> Maxx, Marshall's, and Nordstrom's Rack. I'm
> dressed. I'm believing God for that shopping
> one day.

That's what I wrote.

Earlier, I had thought, *What if I get the news today that I have a donor?* The sun was shining bright. I've completed my exercises well with Colleen's direction. I've walked with Frank around the grounds. I've enjoyed delicious ice cream down the hall from my room on the eighth floor with *Dr. Jeevanandam* and the surgery team. Yes, the surgery team! We had ice cream with all kinds of toppings and enjoyable conversation too! Wow!

I've now received word that my cousin Carolyn was driving my Aunt Norma with husband Kenneth from Washington, DC, arriving in the afternoon tomorrow to visit me. That's 695 miles by car, nearly eleven hours nonstop. My mind was going a mile a minute.

Now, now, that's real special. See, Aunt Norma doesn't care to fly. It would take them only one hour and thirty-nine minutes by air. Uncle Beauford and his wife, Yvonne, had already driven from Atlanta to visit me. That was seven hundred and sixteen miles. That's really, really special. But really, I was thinking, No one *knows exactly how I feel with so many coming to visit and pray for me, encourage me, and bring me gifts that put smile on my face.*

I had shared with Frank earlier how I felt with family and family friends' visits and him being with me every step of the way on this journey. I mean, every step of the way. Their support was making the journey so much easier for me to handle.

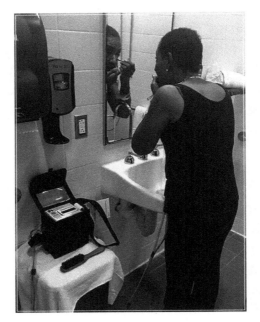

Applying my makeup

I'm looking at myself in the bathroom mirror, applying red MAC Ruby woo lip gloss on my lips, saying to myself, *Self, it's time to get out of here.* But I can't. Wishful thinking again, Pam! Later in the day, my neighbor Pat (this time) brought me some homemade pound cake. After saying thank you, I ate it all. Simply delicious! I had thought of putting a slice away for later. No such luck. All gone!

Pat wrote in my journal:

> We were first neighbors and now friends. I have been blessed to have you in my life. I treasure you as friend. Just know, you are constantly in my prayers and that God answers prayers and he's a healer. With God, all things are possible. I look forward to the four of us having dinner in the Terrance at MCA and listening to jazz.

Family friend Sharon brought me a real large edible arrangement. I love fruit. We shared laughs and Gospel music events together for almost an hour. I remember one day in August when Frank brought me a container filled with watermelon twice. I ate the whole bowl nonstop.

I shared with the great nurses some of my edible arrangement from Sharon after picking off several chocolate-covered bananas, grapes, cantaloupe piece shaped like flowers, and chocolate dipped strawberries. Humm. I wished then for a few warmed oatmeal raisin cookies and more strawberries. This time, covered in Godiva white chocolate. I know that this is just wishful thinking again. Can you imagine what else I was thinking now? Well, if I had this every day, I would be all right while waiting on *a heart.*

It was very nice outside. I looked out the window to my left at another helicopter landing with a patient on the stretcher. I said a prayer for them and a prayer for me. My aunt Norma strutted into my room with her head held high. The expression on her face said a lot to me, "Girl, you are looking good. Isn't God good!"

Kenneth, Norma and Carolyn visited me several days. Then right before they left late Tuesday evening, August 23, 2016, my uncle Kenneth called for prayer.

I should have expected that. He's a *deacon*. He is a *praying man*. It's Aunt Norma, Kenneth, Carolyn, my son John and his wife, Andrea, my grands, Chris and Sheridan, Daphine, Frank, and me. I remember as we connected holding hands. Kenneth prayed and then Frank prayed the most powerful prayer as tears began to flow from our eyes. We felt blessed. It was powerful! Anointed! Blessed! My aunt Norma used to plait my hair when I was up on the Redd's Hill in Saint Albans, West Virginia. I was born in Charleston, West Virginia, some years ago. I loved growing up.

Frank, Pam, Christopher & John

My grandson Chris wrote in my journal:

Dear Grannie,

I hope you are able to get the good news tomorrow and keep your hope always up high! Grannie, I want to see you at your house again. Just like I saw you did one month and thirty days ago. I hope you will feel great tomorrow morning. My mom and my sister love you. My dad and I love you. You are in our prayers. Grannie, we love you!

Wow! I couldn't help but have a good night's rest! The touching prayers and the inspiring music took me into a wonderful sleep after my vitals where taken. The very next morning, the rain was pouring down as I looked outside the window. Nurse Davida rushed into my room and said, "No food. No drink! No food. No drink!" It's exactly 8:00 a.m., I remember, and I will never forget.

Next, Dr. Sarswat rushed into my room and said, "Congratulations, we found the right heart for you!" Frank was on the phone with me hearing her exact words. There were *no words* to describe to you at this point, except reading what the *next* chapter tells you what happens next. Exciting! Magical! *Miracles do happen!*

Chapter 8

Hallelujah! The New Heart Arrives!

Day 26
August 24

The morning of August 24 continued with the news of my *donor's heart* with plenty of excitement in preparation for my surgery. *But the very thing that got me was no food, no drink.* I remember not having *any water*—not even a cherry, orange, grape, blue, or fruity Popsicle. No! A pure fast! I needed something okay, anything.

I remember so well picking up my iPhone, making calls to both sons (John and Kenneth) and various family members. It was a pure thrill like someone winning a lottery or maybe like TV talk show host Oprah's 2004 season opener some years ago when Oprah announced to surprised guests.

"You get a car! You get a car! You get a car! You get a car!" Oprah kept saying it until everyone realized they were getting a car! It was September 13, 2004, when everyone in her studio audience got the news! I was watching that show too.

I didn't get a car. I am getting *a new heart.* Now this was really great! Just great! A donor's heart is a *match!* Hallelujah!

Praise God! You would have had to have been in Room 8011 to know just how the day unfolded.

On my way to the bathroom, I remember cutting a step as though I was stepping with Patrick, my engineer, at the radio station to a Gospel song like artist BeBe Winans' "He Promised Me" or maybe Ricky Dillard's song "Grace" on a Sunday morning during a WVON Broadcast. Yes, it was me and my NuPulseCV iVAS device stepping.

From time to time, I stared in the mirror at myself, saying to myself, *God has been so* good *to me*! Hang in there, Pam! It was time for the preparation of packing up a wardrobe of clothes from home, the slacks, the blouses, and accessories. I had a complete wardrobe in Room 8011. The many get-well cards, books, magazines, and slippers. I remember receiving a large basket full of books, plastic containers, bottles of lotions, slippers, mixed nuts, and spa items from Edward and Doris.

Giving away several floral dish plants to the nurses was easy, and there was much more. It felt good. The nurses were super attentive to me. See, I would not be returning to *that* room anymore. No floral plants close to me for six months after the *new heart*, I was told. I would be in *Intensive Care Unit (ICU)* for several days then assigned to another room on the fourth floor.

Now I look up and see nurse after nurse entering my room saying, *"Congratulations, I told you it would happen!"* I could only smile. They all were so very happy for me. Every single one of them. They were caring, kind, loving, and attentive. They really were my family away from family, it appeared, for twenty-seven days. How do I say thank you (English), gracias (Spanish), even grazie (Italian). I just said thank you repeatedly for the attentiveness and being so knowledgeable.

Several of the nurses attended to the NuPulseCV iVAS patients before me. Remember, I am 004. Now I'm receiving information for the waiting period. It's surely a day of *prep and waiting*. Also, during the wait time, I recalled every nurse, plenty needles, physical examination and special tests like electrocardiograms (EKG) tests, the cardiopulmonary stress tests, chest X-rays, the IV lines, right heart catheterizations, echocardiograms, and walking exercises as well as other tests which determined my *heart function*.

There were many conversations and visitors coming around and so many prayers. In twenty-seven days, I'm on my way to receive a *new heart*. Yes, twenty-seven days! I have a *heart of thanks*, a *heart of gratitude*. Then suddenly, reality sat in. I'm receiving a *new organ* from a person declared *brain dead* due to some *tragic occurrence*. Their organ, blood type, and organ size matched mine. Is it a woman's heart? Is it a man's heart? A young man's heart? And what happened to them? How is the family dealing with the lost?

God, I thank you for the *new heart*, but I wonder about them. *I bless them*. Whomever they may be. I see that the clock on the wall reads 9:00 p.m. The quiet time with Frank was ending. Frank held me in his arms with a very serious look on his face. John has returned. He, Frank, the nurse, and the attendant came to push me as I laid on the stretcher and had arrived in Room 8011. My mind was reflecting all the days behind me.

Now the time had come. We were going from the eighth floor down to the fifth floor. It's time; it's time. I was very optimistic, hopeful, and very prayerful as I tightly held Frank's hand. The doors opened for me to meet the nurses in the *holding* room. They prepared me for the operating room. *Two* or was it *three* doctors spoke to me. Then I talked with the anesthesiologist. I signed papers.

I turned my head to the left and saw Frank. I remember shanking my head back-and-forth. I squeezed Frank's hand. I talked with my pastor, Dr. Horace Smith MD, on my iPhone who had visited me numerous times, and he prayed for me. I spoke to my sister, Pastor Belinda, who called from Atlanta. She prayed for me too.

Then before I'm rolled into the operating room for surgery where the NuPulseCV iVAS device will be *removed* from my body and my *diseased heart* is replaced with a donor's heart, Frank said, "I love you, babe. It's going to be all right. God's got you! Me too!"

In the *next* chapter, read about my *transplant operation* (brace yourself) and about the days that followed.

Chapter 9

The Operation

A beautiful day with plenty of sunshine *would* be my ideal weather as the day continued; however, it's raining. Stormy weather. It's raining hard. The wind was blowing. The trees swaying. But it's okay.

I was thinking back. The day has finally arrived to continue preparations for my *heart transplant*; no doubt about it. It was the *most crucial time* of this journey. Wow! After twenty-seven days in the hospital with the NuPulseCV iVAS device, I was receiving a *new heart*. I feel so incredibly blessed!

I cannot envision what exactly would be happening during the prep time other than what I had read in my "Patients Guide to Heart Transplantation" booklet that I received before entering the University of Chicago Medicine. And, of course, the many questions I've asked. I admit I asked lots of questions. Sometimes, I asked the same question over and over again. It's not easy for me to write about this, not even now.

It was then that I remembered this passage of Scripture, "I will be with you always," and this is what I know for sure, "God is on my side!" I was going to make it through this! My husband, Frank, loves me. *My sons love me.* My family loves me. My circle of close friends loves me. Prayers were going up for me around the country. I feel the prayers. And *I believe in the power of prayer*!

My adorable grandchildren Christopher, Chloe & Sheridan

As I think about just how good *God* has been to me, I think of my grandchildren. I want to see them graduate from elementary and high school and from college.

I want to go to Disney World with my grandchildren. I want to wake up early another morning (again) and take them to school. Suddenly, I was back to reality. I was in the holding area. Doctors were waiting for me. I was in the cotton smock that ties three places in the back; the anesthesiologist inserted some type of IV lines in me to measure my blood pressure and administer medications and fluids. A nurse practitioner or was it the doctors' assistants handling other matters of importance before I was taken to the operating room and put to sleep.

Oh my, oh my. They'd come to take me into the operating room. Many members of the doctors' team greeted me in the operation room. I am asked to slide off the stretcher and onto this bed. I was to place each arm down beside me. I'm asked to turn my head to the left and keep it there. I looked at a rather large square clock on the wall. It's ticking away with red numbers like the NuPulseCV iVAS device that's connected me. It will be removed tonight. I wore it as my friend for twenty-seven days.

I was 004 in the United States of America with the NuPulseCV iVAS device. I remember looking to my left at the clock on the wall. It was after 10:00 p.m. My body was being covered up to my neck. My head was covered with a plastic bag. I'm asked as before what my name is, my birth date, and what am I having done. These questions were also asked each time I was in the operating room for the right heart catheterization.

I had already been asked my favorite songs to play over the sound system. I requested (as before) to start with Hezekiah Walker's famous Gospel song, "Every Praise Belongs to God" into "I Will Survive" to "He Has His Hands on You." I remember singing those songs as voices came through the sound system so loud. I sang every word. The message in each song is very powerful! What I remember next, I had had to gather every thought in my mind a real effective way while singing the words to "I Will Survive." I sure did sing. I wished for a choir to stand around me and sing, but of course, that won't ever happen. You think?

The anesthesia had taken over. I am going out like a light. I am remembering. I'm out! So I'm told during the crucial operation that my damaged *heart* will be removed after my chest is opened about six or more inches to be replaced by the *new heart* sewn in by cardiac surgeon, Dr. Jeevanandam, with his assistants.

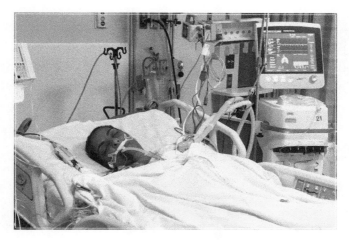

After the transplant

I would be placed on a heart/lung machine. After the heart was sewn in, it would be restarted and then weaned from the heart/lung machine. Then my chest will be sown back up. In recalling these moments, I get the chills.

Next morning after heart transplant

When I woke up the next morning in the intensive care unit (ICU), I had tubes and lines in my body and a breathing tube in my mouth that went down my windpipe and into my lungs. There was a large dressing cloth placed over my chest covering the incision. Three long round tubes were coming out from my chest and the IV lines were inserted in my neck, catheter in my groin, tube in my bladder, and there certainly was more.

But I made it! I made it! I have a *new heart*! Can you imagine this? A new heart! Gospel recording Chicago Mass Choir sang a song entitled "Thank You, Thank You, Jesus," and that's what I say. "Thank you, Thank you Jesus!" I opened my eyes to beautiful music, four and a half hours later in ICU, laying in a long chair that rocked. I couldn't talk. The breathing tube was still in my mouth. I was drowsy. I slightly remember a doctor, Frank, and John were all standing in front of me with a number of nurses from the eighth floor on the side that were with me for twenty-seven days.

I motioned to remove whatever was in my mouth. The doctor removed the tube from my mouth. I couldn't move! I wish I could tell you what happened next other than I closed my eyes. I was knocked out for hours. The morning after the transplantation of my new heart, I remember waking up in the chair with the NuPulseCV iVAS device removed.

I had tubes coming out of me and dressings over the incision where the new heart was placed inside of me. I was stitched up and a dressing placed where the device had been implanted. My neck was bandaged on the right side. I'm remembering correctly six connections from the one needle inserted in my neck. I won't write about my appearance. You don't want to know. But what I know for sure was no makeup, no outfit, and no sandals. I laid in that rocking chair until I was able, later in the evening, to stand and move into the bed. After the three tubes were removed, I was able, with assistance, to walk the hallways. I wore two cotton smocks, of course, they faced two separate ways.

On the fifth day in ICU, I rested. I walked. Then I rested and walked some more. I took many meds taken early in the morning. At noon. At dinner. At night. I stopped counting them. Without an ounce of hesitation, all those meds were taken, it seemed, all day long. There were so many pills. I must have taken nearly three dozen of them. Then there were the blood draws and daily chest X-rays. I know that it was one of the *roughest roads* I have ever traveled, but I made it through into recovery!

Pastor Belinda called me and sang, "I been through the storm and the rain, but I made it. Heart aches and pain, but I made it. This trial, I'm going through, God's going to show you what to do. You can make it."

I felt better when she finished. I kept on singing the song. I'd been moved to another room where I looked up when the door opened, and behind the curtain were my girlfriends from Atlanta, Georgia—Mary and Dion. What a surprise! Mary is very special to me.

In the *next* chapter, you will read why I left Room 4013, returning to ICU. Plus why Mary is so very, very special.

Chapter 10

Something Is Wrong

Day 33
It's August 30

I t's afternoon. I was not sure about the weather today. I didn't
ever remember looking out the window. Mary and Dion were
standing next to me in my room. They will return to Atlanta
tomorrow morning. Mary is a breast cancer survivor. Why is
Mary so very, very, special to me? Some years ago, I *donated* my
hair to Mary. I had long straight thick hair resting on my shoul-
ders. Mary's my friend! I encouraged Mary to hold on!

Pam with long hair in Perugia, Italy

Before returning to Atlanta, Mary wrote in my journal:

"Please take it easy. Take your time in getting better. There is no rush. You are surrounded by family and friends that love you. You are so blessed."

Mary continued writing, "God bless you and may his face shine on you now and always."

It's Friday, September 2. I've gone through three days in July and the entire month of August on the grounds of the University of Chicago Medicine. I'm still here *with my new heart!*

The nurse entered with morning meds. There were lots of them to take.

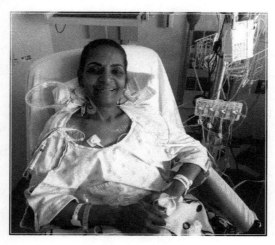

Pam in smock after procedure

She changed my dressings over my *new heart*. She peeped at my stitches right under my collarbone where the incision had been made for the NuPulseCV iVAS device. She paused, then she shared with me that Dr. Adatya had ordered me to return to ICU. *Something was wrong.* Shortly after the nurse left, I *returned* to ICU. My body was struggling to *accept* the *strange object* (my *new heart* is the strange object), and my *numbers* were off, I was told. My numbers were off. Does that mean rejection? I was given blood.

I had had EKGs, blood draws, an MRI, and breathing treatments twice a day by the respiratory therapist. I took loads of meds four times a day. Or was it five times a day? I had lost count. I was in pain with the *numbers* off. It was extremely painful. I'm in Room 4070. I remember, Nurse Chris talked to me. She was very caring and kind. I smiled through my pain, but it was so difficult at times to keep a happy face, praying for my numbers to coincide.

What was going on inside my body puzzled me. I was troubled and concerned. So I prayed. I prayed some more. Those prayers were long and hard. I sang songs. Lots of them. I turned my music up louder on the Kindle.

What's really going on? I really wonder what's really going on. It's Saturday, September 3. I thought I would be home recovering. *I was homesick!* It's real early morning. They won't let me go home. I'm furious. Fuming.

Nothing was moving as I look out the window, save for the clouds passing overhead. I heard a helicopter landing nearby. I turned my head from the window. A nurse walked in to check my vitals. Nurses were constantly in the room for one thing or the other. I had started getting things together in a hurry the moment I thought I was going home. I turned left, looking at the curtain move—and here came Dr. Uriel entering the room at 8:55 a.m. giving me *good* and *sad* news. He said to me, "I was coming along."

Of course, I braced myself. I thought I would be released from the University of Chicago Medicine and would be home recovering. I had hoped to accompany my husband to New Morning Star Church on South Hamlin Boulevard on the West Side in Chicago as he delivered the Sunday morning message. Frank was the guest speaker. Guess what? That did not happen.

I had to stay in the hospital. I was speechless. I dropped my head in disappointment. I was so sad.

I also thought I would be attending the African Festival of the Arts in Washington Park, Labor Day Weekend that opened the day before today on Friday, September 2. This African Festival of arts has vibrant drumming all day at the Drum Village. Collectible artifacts, colorful and rich handwoven fabric and textile, and an African marketplace. I love the many vendors, nearly three hundred of them. The African jewelry and gorgeous attire and the cravings, I looked forward to them too. The musical nightly program is always so exciting. Well, guess what? That didn't happen either. Tempting as it was, I could only see the festival from my hospital window.

I really was more than disappointed. It was Labor Day Weekend, and I was still in the hospital. Dr Uriel stated during his visit that I would have a *biopsy* the following Monday. That's the Monday after next Sunday that Frank will minister at New Morning Star Church. Do you know what that meant? That meant *another full week* in the University of Chicago Medicine.

Oh no! No! They won't let me go home! You should have seen the look on my face. I was bummed. I wished I could hear Frank deliver the message. I was very sad. Dr. Uriel knew that. "Another week, Pam," he said.

That morning, I came up with every excuse in the book to get released to go home. Do you understand what I am saying? I even remember saying, "Dr. Uriel, I live less than fifteen minutes from the University of Chicago Medicine. I could return in case of any emergency." I gave the route from home to the hospital. *Nothing* worked. *Absolutely nothing.* You should have heard me. You would have thought I was trying to sell a product for a company, putting finishing touches on closing a deal.

Valerie (one of my goddaughters) had flown from Atlanta to visit. She prayed with me, and we talked. Went shopping during her visit for me. Valerie arrived bearing gifts. One was a small bronze-colored cross that I could squeeze in my hands during blood draws. I needed that. Valerie brought me two plaques with incredible, thoughtful readings.

One of them read: "Don't worry about tomorrow. God is already there." The other read: "Life is not measured by the *number* of *breaths* we take but by the moments *that take our breath away."*

That very night, Val and I prayed. Val did the same thing Beverly did. She bent her head, looked me in the eyes, grabbed both of my hands, and oh, did we pray. We called on the name of the Lord for the *numbers* in my body to regulate. We called on the name of Jesus until tears started running down out of both of our eyes.

I read those plaques every day and sometimes twice a day, if not three times a day to encourage my *heart*!

That very night, Val prayed again for me. We ended up calling on the name of Jesus together for the numbers to regulate. We called Jesus until tears ran down both of our eyes. It reminded me of Thursday night worship services in West Virginia up on the Redd's Hill, which I described in my introduction and I loved that hill. I remember growing up in *Saint Albans, West Virginia*, where my aunt Mabel would play the piano and took lead every time on "Call on Jesus, He'll Answer Prayer." That song was sung in many services repeatedly. I wish *you* could have met my aunt Mabel. Everybody should have one.

This incredible woman of God was smart, caring, compassionate, cordial, courageous, thoughtful, charming, and one of the greatest inspirations in my life. My aunt Mabel was my backbone. I can tell you that I learned more from her than anyone else I've ever known. She taught me how to cook, drive, sing, and be a real a real child of God. She taught and motivated me to read the Bible every day. Her life on this earth made a difference in my life. I'm grateful she was in my life. Here I was now years later as a heart transplant patient.

I was wearing the heart monitor that's hooked up to me with electrodes placed on my chest held together by adhesive glue to record my heart activity. From day one (July 28), I had had the heart monitor attached to me. So it's time to go to sleep. I was having difficulty sleeping. I wanted to go home and make some cherry Jell-O.

All I had to do is add one cup of boiling water to gelatin mix, stir for two minutes, and add one cup of cold water until completely dissolved. Place in the refrigerator until firm. But I can't do that. Now my Aunt Mabel would sprinkle a little sugar in her Jell-O. Maybe that's worth trying. My *new heart* would love it. You think?

In the *next* chapter, read what the *next two weeks* were like, especially when I choose not to sleep in the bed for three nights but on the couch with four pillows under me and more family surprises that encouraged *my heart* and made me smile.

Chapter 11

A Joyful Recovery

September 4

Early autumn. I was up. I was dressed in black slacks and black-and-white silk blouse with a black camisole while sitting in my chair going nowhere—streaming Sunday morning worship service at Apostolic Faith Church. I wished I was sitting in the second pew participating in the worship experience with others.

Dr. Uriel has visited me. He saw my pastor, Dr. Horace Smith MD, ministering the Gospel. He watched a few minutes with me. It's inside the 8:00 a.m. hour. From the smile on Dr. Uriel's' face—he's enjoying it too. He knew I wish I was there!

My *biopsy* wasn't scheduled until Monday, September 12. What was I doing here? I wanted to recover at home. I wanted nothing else but to go home. These long, agonizing weeks in the hospital have taken their toll on me. I was not as nice as I had always been. The real main reason was, I was ready to go *home*. See, every morning, I thought about home. But everything had to be working right. I've moved to Room 4028. My sister, Pastor Belinda, and her husband, Walter, surprised me with a visit from Atlanta. We hugged. We prayed. We ate together.

Pastor Belinda wrote in my journal:

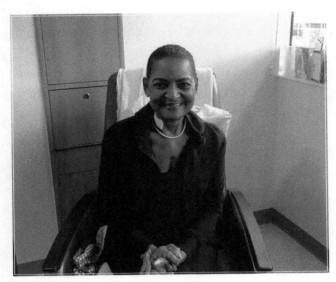

Pam in black sweat suit with pearls, room 4028

"I have just witnessed a wonderful miracle! My sister Pam has beat the odds, and I have seen God's love! Thank you for loving me with both of your hearts."

I kept thinking back to what's still going on continuously with me. Morning meds, meds, and then more meds. EKG, MRI, stress tests, chest X-rays, and blood draws (needles, needles, needles). Then Nurse Daveth brought more meds, breathing treatments, and vitals.

I remembered one day (or was it two days?) when I wanted to toss the pills across the room, but during my uncle Beauford's visit, we walked through the hallways, I remember him telling me, "Whatever you do, take your medications, every one."

I responded, "Okay! I will. Every one of them." I listened to my WVON broadcast. It really inspired me! The music is blessed. Gives you hope! I loved it and still love it. Val, my goddaughter, departed for Atlanta.

Val wrote in my journal:

> This is the day that the Lord has made. Let us rejoice and be glad in it. Pam, I am glad to see you and how God is healing you. God heard your cry and dried your tears from your eyes. He sent you a new heart! What a mighty God we serve! I am so happy to see you up and full of life and strength with your black warm-up suit, pearl necklace, and earrings. We prayed and had a praise party today. Pam, keep doing good.

The week ended with four more dear family friends from Los Angeles, California, surprising me with a very delightful visit by Joyce and Leon and Larry and Leeadda. I sang over thirty-eight years ago in Los Angeles at Larry and Leeadda's wedding. (I didn't remember that.) She did. Joyce and Larry are sisters and brothers and a part of my life nearly forty years! We hugged. We hugged some more. What an incredible visit.

We shared conversations from our past. I believe true friends are life's greatest blessing. We talked about the trip we had together. They were special holiday gatherings, worship services, shopping excursions, and so much more. I'm so blessed!

While Leeadda and Daphine went across the street walking through the DuSable Museum of African American History, I told Joyce that I actually had gone an entire month without cooking a meal and folding up clothes after washing. Watering my gorgeous red prayer plant, my palm plant, my aloe vera plant, and shopping, especially with at TJ Maxx, Marshall's, HomeGoods, Nordstrom Rack, Hobby Lobby, Sam's Club, and Costco.

I said that life in the hospital was so much different from life at home. I was taken away from everything that mattered to me. Joyce comforted me with great words. When Joyce, Larry, Leon, and Leeadda left to have dinner, it made me smile to see them return with dinner for me. Along with Frank, we all gathered together on the seventh floor right over from the sky lobby and dined together. So special. Family Friends!

It's Day 45 in the hospital. That day was September 11. I remember the temperature had gone from a hot steamy and humid summer days to a taste of autumn. I was still here in the University of Chicago Medicine sitting in a large dark grey chair signing a document for Monday morning's right heart catheterization.

I also remember on September some eleven years ago. It was 2001. A very terrible and horrible situation happened in New York City to the Twin Towers of the World Trade Center. The Pentagon was hit. A plane crashed in a field in Pennsylvania. Nearly three thousand people including firefighters, paramedics, and police officers' lives were lost. But here I was with life God has given me—another chance at *life*. I remember that day and prayed for the families. I called on the *name of Jesus!*

Day 46

It's Monday at 5:08 a.m.

I wrote in my journal:

Abc7chicago Tracy Butler weather update: "It's a day of beauty. Dry and comfy start with possible showers expected later in the week." I smiled.

I was dressed in the cotton smock and was being taken to the operating room on a stretcher for my scheduled biopsy. Later, Dr. Uriel visited and said, "It went well!" But we had to wait for full results that must read 1A or 0. We waited.

On Day 47, September 13, Nurse Ola did my blood draw and told me to hold on! He further said, "You'll be going home soon. I feel it."

"I sure hope so," I replied.

It seemed to be long days, not much activity. I waited. My loving and caring husband, Frank, wrote in my journal:

> Through God's grace, you (we) have come a long way. This journey has not been easy, but God's grace has blessed each step. Pam, you have strong faith and it continues to sustain you. Your coming home will be good. Just let the process work and maintain the faith you have. I love you and will continue to be with you each step. The best is yet to come.
>
> Love,
> Frank

Inside Day 48, I wrote in my journal:

> It's 4:15 a.m., Wednesday. I fell asleep last night watching ministers minister including the late Bishop G. E. Patterson and my pastor, Dr. Horace Smith MD, videos again. I feel blessed and favored by God. I have a *new heart* and a *chance at life again.*

Day 49 was behind the curtain. September 15, Thursday. It's around 3:00 a.m. I woke up with tears in my eyes. I waited on the blood draw, meds, and morning vitals. I was sleeping under four pillows on the couch because I had had enough of the bed. I didn't want to do anything with the bed but look at it. I did.

Then words of a song written in the year of 1945 by pianist songwriter and lyricist Alma Bazel Androzzo made famous by Mahalia Jackson came into my heart, "If I can help somebody as I pass along, if I can help somebody with a word or a song. If I can show somebody that he's traveling wrong, then my living shall not be in vain." I want to live, and I want to go *home*. I wasn't discharged as expected and was so sad but thankful to be blessed with a *new heart*.

Dr. Jeevanandam described my *new heart* again during his visit in middle September, "You will take care of that Tesla heart with a ludicrous upgrade." Then he smiled. We continued with a brief conversation before turning to leave from my room.

So just in case you are wondering, a Tesla is an impressive car. It's one of the most outstanding automobiles on the high-way that stands out as the only true electric luxury sedan. It has tremendous wicked quick acceleration cutting-edge tech. Potential range is three hundred plus miles. The Tesla can sprint from zero to sixty miles per hour in just 2.5 seconds, I'm told. I have *a Tesla heart*! Wow!

In my *next* and *last* chapter, read about *my last* week at the University of Chicago Medicine. *Why!* I screamed (again) on September 22 at 10:30 a.m. Plus I am advised what not to eat anymore and what to eat more of.

Chapter 12

Going Home

Hallelujah! It turned out to be my last week in the University of Chicago Medicine (hospital) even though I've said from the beginning I didn't ever see this happening to me in the first place. One must be strong to make it this long in one place.

Listen, *there is nothing* I really want more at the time than to go home! It's Sunday, September 18. I was up and dressed in a two-piece black jogging warm-up suit with my pearls. My blood was drawn again. I didn't have to be in a hurry to go anywhere.

Dressed sitting in the chair

I've taken my morning meds, and my vitals were completed. After putting on my makeup, I had slipped into my gold-wedged sandals. For breakfast, I had ordered two broiled eggs, a fruit cup, and oatmeal with raisins and extra brown sugar plus cranberry and orange juice. Still, I was *totally* frustrated just because I wanted to go home. Yet I was still in the hospital but thankful.

I was sitting up in the chair. I completed writing two boxes of *thank you* notes to express heartfelt thanks for the many greetings cards I received, plants, and gifts. I had read my daily Word and turned every page in the People's magazine Daphine had brought me.

> I remember so distinctly, thinking back, when the respiratory therapist walked into the room, and looked for the patient, said to me after entering from behind the pulled curtain, "I will come back for her." I smiled, then I immediately responded by pulling the black sleeve on my left arm up to my elbow and then showed him my white write band. You should have seen his face. I believe he thought, I was a visitor, not the patient.

I reached over to my left and then picked up my journal and started to read what my eldest son John wrote:

> I never thought I would be given the opportunity to wash your hair. These new experiences are the moments that last for a lifetime. Another reason you push through your fears. Mom, when you doubt and your thoughts seem convoluted trust the souls that love

you. A new heart is a new start! You are not at
the finish line because God said I have more
for you to see, feel, touch, do, and hear. I am
here, Mom. I've always been here, working to
make you proud of me. I love you.

My son John washes my hair. Yes, these experiences last a
lifetime. It felt good. Very, very, very special! I was being told
my biopsy is scheduled on Wednesday, September 21, at 8 a.m.
and that they *will* give me a discharge date. I hoped. I prayed for
remarkable results like never before. One thing I knew was how
to pray. All I really could do was to pray. Then I started praying again. No need for a jacket in the autumn weather, no sun-
glasses and no high heel pumps. I was inside where I've listened
to incredible moving, touching, and powerful music every day—
music that has inspired me. I am away from the outside world.

An American music executive named Clarence Avant from
Climax, North Carolina, once said, "I can't imagine a world
without music!" I'm thinking, *Me either.*

This incredible singer and Emmy award winner and a fam-
ily friend, Joan, visited me. She encouraged me too. In August,
Joan had brought me a plate of delicious home cooked food.
Joan had me smiling. She made me want to lick the plate.

Now speaking of dinner, I remember Daphine bringing
me lemon chicken and baked potato with steamed broccoli
from Millers Pub twice. Daphine kept delivering Kettle potato
chips, Garrett's popcorn, pure leaf raspberry tea, and was that
all? I'll never tell.

I remember sending Daphine to the sky lobby for a cup
of soup on many occasions, sandwiches more times than I can
recall. Special persons, special good deeds. Didn't Tyler Perry
produce, direct, and star in a movie called "Good Deeds" in

February 2012? Yes, it was, and I went to see it. Three times, I believe.

It's still Sunday, four days and several hours from the telephone call that had me *screaming l*ouder than a two-month-old baby getting a needle shot in her arm loud enough for two nurses to come rushing in my room at the same time, asking, "Are you okay? Are you okay?" Well, let me tell you shortly about that.

I wrote in my journal:

> It's 7 a.m. My meds are down. Morning meds, that is. Blood drawn. Vitals. I'm dressed, sitting in my chair in Room 4028, feeling good and blessed and waiting on next step. It's Sunday. I can't go to church nor WVON!

On WVON Radio, I listened to my program. There were great, moving songs, even my voice. Frank had pre-recorded me earlier in my hospital room. I was taken away from what I love because I needed a *new heart.* I still—was—very blessed while listening.

In August (not sure which day it was), I called my girlfriend Beverly to share my sentiments for her kindness. Bev said, "Whenever, you are discharged from the hospital, come stay in my home for a week as you continue to recover."

So let me go back and pick up where I left off with what happened after Sunday, September 18.

It's early Monday morning. At 4:45 a.m., I was up, dressed like I am going to church with my makeup on and ready for blood draw, and it was before 5:00 a.m. Vitals came next. I was ready. Why not be ready?

I was sitting on the corner of the couch, listening to Shirley Horn's inspiring song "Here's to Life" when phlebotomist Leonne came from behind the curtain saying, "One more time, angel." I got up and sat on the edge of the bed, thinking, *Another blood draw?*

A *phlebotomist* draws blood. She filled five tubes of my blood, shaking them from the left to right before placing in the tray. Then I laid back down until time for my morning meds. I had to learn how to get along with all my pills. I began seven days earlier—taking meds with pure leaf raspberry tea. It's very good!

I wrote in my journal:

Dressed and planning to go home

"Two more procedures, hopefully. I pray will go well. God is able! God is good! God is amazing! Because I'm ready to go home!"

It's Tuesday, September 20, 2016. It's thirty-five minutes past midnight. See—I can't go to sleep. So I wrote and wrote and wrote some more. Then I watched more sermon videos of my pastor, Dr. Horace Smith MD, Pastor Frank Thomas, and Bishop G. E. Patterson Minister. It's like they were talking directly to me. Maybe they were. Nurse Mia stepped in to check on me. My ceiling light was still on. See, my room was right in front of the nurses' station.

I looked over to my left as she entered the room. Guess what I said, "I want to go home."

"I know, I know you will. Can I get you anything?" she said. Then she said, "I can only imagine your pain and what you are going through."

I said, "No, you can't. You have not been where I am. No, no," I said.

Mia smiled and turned away, leaving from my room. Earlier, I had completed one of two scheduled tests. I was told that my echocardiogram results were good. The biopsy was next. It's on Wednesday, September 21. So a *biopsy is* an examination of tissue removed from a living body to discover the presence, cause, or extent of a disease.

And an *echocardiogram* is a test of the action of the heart using ultrasound waves to produce a visual display monitoring of heart disease.

I talked out loud to myself, "Must keep a positive attitude. I must continue to walk the hallways. I'm feeling remarkably blessed. Numbers so far look good." So here I was, all excited and another nurse was just talking. No updated news on discharge, just more meds plus the biopsy wasn't until Wednesday. I was thinking, *Has it been canceled? No way, it's got to happen.* Breathing treatment happened with the respiratory therapist again.

While exchanging conversation and making direct eye contact, I said, "I want to go home."

"You will and soon. I believe it. I pray for you," she said. She continued by saying, "Angel, I'm not the only one praying for you." Later in the afternoon, my friend Santrice from *American Heart Association* (where I once served as a volunteer, an emcee for their Gospel concert) visited me and wrote in my journal:

"You have touched so many people, and God decided he wanted you to touch so many more people, and so he gave you life twice! Go out and be that light! You are a true blessing! *God favors you.*" So very *special!* Another delightful visit and conversation.

It's Wednesday, September 21. At 4:00 a.m., Nurse Erika walked in my room to check my vitals. She told me that my blood will be drawn at 5:00 a.m. She asked me how I feel. By now, every nurse and the doctors know how I feel.

My biopsy was scheduled at 7:00 a.m. How could I forget? I was ready at 6:00 a.m. with the smock on tied in three knots in the back. I had switched from my night gown to the smock. Yes, I was wearing the cotton smock.

The smock must be brought into my room because I didn't like the smock in my room. I didn't. Maybe it was a mind issue; however, I was praying it was my last time wearing one. God sure answers prayers. It turned out to be the last time I wore the *smock.* Almost the entire day after returning to my room, I was quiet. Yes, yes, I prayed and I prayed and I prayed. See, I *strongly believe* in the power of prayer.

I thought back to the many kind, incredible, loving, efficient, attentive, and caring nurses and nurse assistants that *included* Katie, Geraldine, DaVita, Stephanie, Sue, Margo, Mia, Ta-Aqua, Mylanda, two different Lauras and Meagans, and the four male nurses Ola, Mike, Mark, and Curtis—for the incredible healthcare they had given to me hour by hour, day after day, and week after week, at the University of Chicago Medicine.

Then I thought of the days of excruciating pain experienced in my body, *pain you would not wish on anyone*. Not anyone no matter who they were. Did I share with you that it was my late aunt Mabel who visited me in the spirit world many days earlier and said, "Get up and get dressed."?

I was thinking, *I'm in the hospital. Where am I going?* I got up. Into the bathroom I went. Got dressed. I sat in the chair not that far from my bed. My attitude was better dressed even if I wasn't going anywhere.

Finally it's Thursday, September 22. Today perhaps this is the day for good biopsy news, so I can be discharged and go home! You think? I was not remembering my breakfast order. It was probably some sort cereal, a banana, apple sauce, and cranberry and orange juice. Like previous orders.

What I remember distinctly was, it's exactly 10:30 a.m., as I looked at the clock on the wall. The phone rang. It's my transplant coordinator Tiana on the other end. Tiana said hello to me, "I have your biopsy results. It's 0 rejection! I am working on your discharge papers, so you can go home!"

I literally screamed, "Thank you, Jesus. Thank you Jesus!" Oh my God. Thank you." I was loud! Nurses rushed in my room, saying, "You okay? I know. I know. You're going home." I was already packed and ready! Another *surprise* visit moments later was from our dear family friend who flew in from New Orleans, Louisiana, Dr. Gloria Jackson Bacon. So very special.

Dr. Bacon wrote in my journal:

> My dearest Pam, I am so delighted to be sitting here with you as you pack to leave this place today! It is such a joy to know you and share your joy of living and loving God. I glory in the joy that your Faith brings. I am

so happy that Frank is the love of your life!
May God continue to bless you both.

Several hours later, Frank arrived. Frank filled another engagement for me that I couldn't make. We hugged with tears in my eyes and arms wrapped around each other. I said, "Babe, I'm going home!" It was like I have received the best news in the world. Guess what? I did. I'm going home!

After signing of the discharge papers, Frank gathered my things, and I finally left the hospital after going down the elevator. So, yes, I gladly sat in the wheelchair. The car was there. Frank opened the passenger's backseat door on the right side for me to sit. That's where I would be sitting for three months in any automobile.

Was Frank going to be driving Mrs. Daisy now? (I remember the movie *Driving Miss Daisy*, December 1989). My three months in the backseat would be longer than that movie was in the theater near you or me! But that was okay. No problem.

I would not fly for six months. I couldn't have lived flowers or plants in our home for months. I would wear a surgical face mask whenever outside for three months, even to church. It was okay with me! Home is my place to be as I recover, and that's fine with me! My containers of meds were with me, plenty of them in a black divided pill box marked by days and hours. I had started taking after the heart transplant up to thirty-eight meds a day.

At the time of this writing and nearly two years later, I went down to eight meds a day. Weekly return visits to the hospital for biopsies, blood draws, and echograms plus, but that's okay. I'm going home! I will go from weekly to monthly to quarterly visits. But God would see me through! My diet changed. No more eating grapefruits. I couldn't have a half a glass of grapefruit juice. (I had loved grapefruits!) No pomegranates. No blood red oranges. Thoroughly cooked foods. Eat hard boiled eggs, not over easy anymore (like I used to love them).

I continue *eating healthy* with a balanced diet. Meds have scheduled times for intake all throughout each day every day. Much protein and exercise weren't going to be a problem. I had always enjoyed walking. As we arrive downstairs to exit the University of Chicago Medicine, I wanted the fastest way possible home in the most expeditious manner.

I said that our automobile was sitting there. Frank drove south from the medical center then north down Lake Shore Drive turning right off 31st Street exit and left on King Drive to 26th Street to arrive at our home, and all I could say while sitting in the backseat was, "Hallelujah. Thank you, Jesus. I know what prayer can do!" With each day, I got better and better. I knew I was a walking blessed miracle!

So blessed, so very blessed with the gift of hope. Exactly sixteen months and twenty-seven days after my heart transplant in January 2018, Gift of Hope arranged two meetings; where I looked into the donor's mother and father's face and said, "Thank you! Thank you! Thank you! Thank you! Thank you! You have given me life through your son."

And *all* she wanted was hear her son's *heartbeat*. We were handed the stethoscope that was placed to her ears, and tears flowed down both of our faces as we held on to each other; and she heard her son's heartbeat sounding in me. *What a moment! What a moment! An unforgettable moment!* The donor's son's organs saved six lives. Wow! I am one of them today! Here I am. Happy. Living my life. A blessed child of God! A walking miracle! God is amazing! Awesome. He's good! Prayer works!

And, yes, it's a song.

> I don't feel no ways tired come too far from
> where I started from

Nobody told me the road would be easy
I don't believe He brought me this far to
leave me"

(Words written by Curtis Burrell and performed by the
late famous Gospel singer/artist Rev. James Cleveland).

With all *my heart*, I say, please consider becoming a *donor*!
Give the gift of life! The gift of hope! Hallelujah! Save a life! I
honor you!

Epilogue

*N*ow I'm quite sure you wondered just how I'm doing. How things turned out after leaving the University of Chicago Medicine on September 22, 2016, especially if you do not have the pleasure (as so many have) to listen to my WVON Sunday broadcast where I give every listener every broadcast updates on my health. I'm doing so well! No rejection! No infection to my heart! Feeling blessed! I thank God every day!

Pam at WVON radio

Secondly, I took my friend Beverly up on her invitation. I stayed with her for several days, giving Frank a much-needed break. Shopped at Stein Mart, DSW, TJ Maxx, Marshall's, and Hobby Lobby during my stay!

(I took my *meds* with me to Beverly's home remembering Frank sharing with Beverly that Pam must take her meds every morning, afternoon, and night).

And it's not that exciting to share with you that the day I was released to fly (again) in February 2017, I would be up in the air on Southwest Airlines headed to New York to *speak* at my late uncle Bill's Home going service in Long Island. He prayed for me. Also, I was excited to *plan* for the next weeks, months, and the next year with my loving husband, Frank.

I've taken my grandchildren to school, and we've enjoyed Disney Springs in Orlando, Florida! I've been to DuSable Museum of African American History (several more times), the African Festival of the Arts, and rode the Ferris Wheel at Navy Pier.

And as for meds, there are certain ones I will be on for the rest of my life. I take them daily every twelve hours. I have life! I am down from weekly biopsies to quarterly doctor visits to annual visits and blood draws at the clinic as I keep in touch with my *transplant coordinator who will shadow me the rest of my life*. I am driving everywhere. I'm shopping (at my favorite places). I'm going to *church* every Sunday! I'm living an intentional life!

On this remarkable journey of my life, I am feeling blessed and happy *every day*. I laugh! I do not try to beat the clock remembering tomorrow is another day. I take time to rest, recharge, and regroup. I say yes to life!

Every Sunday on my WVON radio program, I have a saying that I leave with you, "I love you, and there's absolutely nothing you can do about it!"

And, yes, meeting the donor family was a very, very special time in my life. We keep in contact. I believe in God! Someone saved my life! Become a donor! Save a life! Enjoy life! Live! This is my story!